THE

ORIGIN OF THE ROYAL ARCH

ORDER OF MASONRY,

HISTORICALLY CONSIDERED;

INCLUDING

AN EXPLANATORY VIEW OF ITS PRIMITIVE

RITUALS, DOCTRINES, AND SYMBOLS,

And of their Progressive Improvements to the present time.

REV. GEORGE OLIVER, D. D.

PAST GRAND COMMANDER OF THE 33° FOR ENGLAND AND WALES;
PAST P.G.M. OF THE GRAND LODGE OF MASSACHUSETTS;
PAST D.P.G.M. FOR LINCOLNSHIRE;
AND HONORARY MEMBER OF NUMEROUS LODGES AND LITERARY SOCIETIES.

"Difficile est propriè communia dicere."
HOR. DE ART. POET. 128.

A NEW EDITION,
WITH
A MEMOIR OF THE AUTHOR.

Cornerstone Book Publishers
New Orleans, LA
2013

Origin of the Royal Arch

A Cornerstone Book
Published by Cornerstone Book Publishers
An Imprint of Michael Poll Publishing
Copyright © 2013 by Cornerstone Book Publishers

Cornerstone Book Publishers
New Orleans, LA

Photographic reprint of the 1867 edition
First Cornerstone Edition - 2013

www.cornerstonepublishers.com

ISBN: 1613420730
ISBN-13: 978-1-61342-073-7

MADE IN THE USA

Analytical Table of Contents.

—◦◦—

PART I.

THE ORIGIN OF THE ROYAL ARCH HISTORICALLY CONSIDERED.

CHAPTER I.

THE YORK GRAND LODGE.

CONTENTS.

CONTENTS.

CONTENTS.

CONTENTS.

PART II.

PROGRESSIVE RITUALS, DOCTRINES, AND SYMBOLS OF THE ROYAL ARCH.

CHAPTER I.

THE FIRST ROYAL ARCH RITUAL.

CONTENTS.

CHAPTER II.

THE SECOND DIVISION OF THE PRIMITIVE RITUAL.

CONTENTS.

CHAPTER III.

THE TESTIMONY OF ST. JOHN THE EVANGELIST.

CHAPTER IV.

THE EXCELLENT AND SUPER-EXCELLENT DEGREES.

CONTENTS.

CHAPTER V.

BRO. DUNCKERLEY'S RITUAL.

CHAPTER VI.

THE SEAL OF SOLOMON.

CONTENTS.

CHAPTER VII.

AN OLD ROYAL ARCH TRACING-BOARD EXEMPLIFIED.

CHAPTER VIII.

THE TETRAGRAMMATON.

CONTENTS.

CHAPTER IX.

THE INSIGNIA.

CONTENTS.

CHAPTER X.

SYMBOLS.

THE ORIGIN OF THE
ENGLISH ROYAL ARCH DEGREE.

---◦◦◦---

PART I.

THE ORIGIN OF THE ROYAL ARCH
HISTORICALLY CONSIDERED.

CHAPTER I.

THE YORK GRAND LODGE.

THERE are in Speculative Freemasonry several problems *sub judice*, which have exercised the ingenuity of the Brethren in all ages of its existence. Such as, whether Freemasonry was introduced into Europe by the gypsies ?[1]—Whether it can be correctly identified with Rosicrucianism ?[2]

---

[1] Mr. Clinch boldly affirms the fact. The opinion is repeated in De Pauw's Egypt. This author observes, " Every person who was not guilty of some public crime could obtain admission to the lesser mysteries. Those vagabonds called Egyptian priests in Greece and Italy, required considerable sums for initiation ; and their successors the gypsies practise similar mummeries to obtain money. And thus was Freemasonry introduced into Europe."

[2] There is an Essay in the *London Magazine* for January, 1824, to prove the identity of Freemasonry and Rosicrucianism, and their modern origin ; and the writer concludes that " though Rosicrucianism is not Freemasonry, yet the latter borrowed its form from the former." An American anti-Mason endeavours to propagate the same opinion. He says, "the Rosicrucian mania sprung up in Germany A.D. 1610, and nearly overspread Christendom. This puff of indefinable extravagance originated from the writings of John Valentine Andrea, a celebrated theologian of Wurtemburg, who amused himself with tales of spiritual wonder and of mystical glory, as a literary hoax, in the style of Baron Munchausen's wonderful adventures. The visionary minds of that day took his work in earnest. They claimed for

—Whether it be, or how it is, connected with the
Templars? [3] who, as some think, received it from
the Druses of Mount Lebanon.[4]—Whether the
numerous foreign degrees, called Ecossais, were
really derived from Scotland? [5] &c.   And as the

the Rosy Cross philosophy what is now particularly claimed for
Freemasonry." It is believed in Germany that Freemasonry
originated with the Rose Croix. The Baron de Gleichen says
that the Masons were united with the Rose Croix in England
under King Arthur. I suppose he considers the Knights of the
Round Table to be of this Order. The Baron de Westerode
gives as his opinion that the Rose Croix was promulgated in
the eastern parts of Europe in 1188 for the propagation of
Christianity, and that it was received in Scotland under the
appellation of the Order of Eastern Masons, and contained the
secrets of all the occult sciences, and that it found its way into
England in 1196; that it consisted of three degrees, and its
emblems were a pair of golden compasses suspended from a
white ribbon, as a symbol of purity and wisdom ; the sun, the
moon, a double triangle with the letter א ; and the Brethren
wore a gold ring, with the initials I. A. A. T. (Ignis, Aer,
Aqua, Terra).

[3] Ramsay, Hunde, and many other innovators, founded their
systems on the postulate that Freemasonry was a branch of
Templary. Barruel was very positive on this point, and all the
arguments which he has used to vilify Freemasonry in his
" History of Jacobinism " are expressly founded upon it.

[4] This figment, I believe, has been adopted by the editor of
the *Christian Remembrancer.*

[5] It is curious to observe how diversified the seventy degrees
of the so-called Scotch Masonry are ; and I subjoin a catalogue
of them for the information of the curious Mason :—Novice
Ecossais ; Maître Ecossais ; Parfait Ecossais ; Parfait Maître
Anglais Ecossais ; Ecossais Parisien ; Rite Ecossais ; Ecossais
Anglais ou des Frères aînés ; Ecossais Rouge ; Ecossais d'Angle-
terre ; Ecossais de Lyon ; Grand Ecossais ; Ecossais Français ;
Chevalier Ecossais ; Ecossais Trinitaire ; Parfait Ecossais ;
Ecossais Trinitaire, ou Globe des Grand Maîtres Commandeurs

solution of these problems depends upon evidence
which is inaccessible, it admits of considerable
doubt whether they will ever be elucidated with
such absolute precision as to merit universal
credence.

But the most important question which remains
open at the present day, is the true origin of the
English Royal Arch. The enquiry has excited
much attention, and a great anxiety appears to

de Temple ; Ecossais Trinitaire, ou puissant Grand Maître de
l'Ordre de la Sainte Trinité ; Ecossais Sublime Anglais ; Ecossais
d'Alcidony ; Ecossais de Montpellier ; Ecossais de Paris ; Ecossais de Dunkerque ; Ecossais Egyptien ; Ecossais de Prusse ;
Ecossais de Messine ; Ecossais de Naples ou de Sicile ; Ecossais
d'Angers ; Ecossais de Clermont ; Ecossais Architecte parfait ;
Ecossais de l'Anneau ; Ecossais de Heredom ; Grand Architecte Ecossais ; Grand Architecte Anglais Ecossais ; Ecossais
fideles ou de la Vieille Bru ; Grand Patriarche Ecossais ; Grand
Ecossais de Saint André d'Ecosse ; Ecossais de Saint André
d'Ecosse ; Ecossais de Saint André du Chardon ; Grand Ecossais
Patriarche ; Grand Ecossais des Patriarches ; Illustre Architecte
Ecossais ; Sublime Ecossais de la G. L. du Prince Edward ;
Sublime Ecossais, ou la Jerusalem céleste ; Ecossais de St.
Georges ; Ecossais Purificateur ; Ecossais de Toulouse ; Ecossais
Vert ; Ecossais Sublime Purificateur ; Ecossais des Quarante ;
Ecossais des petits apartemens ; Ecossais des fils ainés ; Ecos-
sais de Franville ; Ecossais de la Quarantine ; Ecossais des trois
j.j.j. (inconnus) ; Grand Ecossais, ou Grand Elu ; Rite Ecossais
philosophique ; Grand Ecossais des Croisades ; Ecossais des
Freres ainés, ou du Triple Triangle ; Ecossais d'Hiram ; Grand
Maître Ecossais ; Ecossais de la Loge du Prince Edward, G. M. ;
Ecossais Levite et Martyr ; Grand Ecossais de Valachie, de
Copenhagen et de Stockholm, ou Grade de l'Interieur ; Ecossais
de la Voûte sacrée de Jacques VI. ; Ecossais des Loges mili-
taires ; Ecossais de St. André ; Ecossais de St. André, ou quatre
fois respectable Maître ; Ecossais de la perfection ; Dame
Sublime Ecossaise ; Ecossais de l'Hospice du Mont Thabor.

prevail amongst the Companions of the Order to ascertain truly the fact whether it be an ancient or a modern rite. The Ahiman Rezon says it has been held "from time immemorial;" but this is rather an indefinite expression, and somewhat difficult to comprehend. Some have asserted more determinately that the Templars brought it from the Holy Land; others that it was attached as a pendant to Templary in the sixteenth century; and some believe that it was unknown before the year 1780. There exists sufficient evidence to disprove all these conjectures, and to fix the error of its introduction to a period which is coeval with the memorable schism amongst the English Masons about the middle of the last century. To ascertain the causes which gradually led to its establishment, we must take a brief view of the leading circumstances attending that division of the Fraternity into two great and independent bodies.

It is commonly believed that the prevalence of schism in any institution is the fruitful parent of many evils, which cannot fail to detract from its purity and excellence. And so it is; but the evil is not without its portion of good. Experience teaches that if the members of an institution become apathetic, nothing is so likely to rouse them to a sense of duty as the existence of conflicting opinions, which produce a separation of interests, and divide them into two adverse sections; each of which, like the self-multiplying polypus, will frequently become as strong and prosperous as the parent institution. This is peculiarly the case in religion. Separation, and the establishment of new sects, have generally been a prolific source of proselytism; and many a Christian may trace his conversion from a state resembling the darkest heathenism to the spirit of party, and the curiosity of searching for something new, stimulating, and attractive. In Freemasonry, from the same causes, former feelings are revived and brought into operation, which enliven the lukewarm zeal, and convert the most quiescent member into an active partizan. Like a gentle breeze directed on the embers of an expiring fire, schism fans the dying apathy of the inert, and gives a new impetus to his thoughts, words, and actions.

Some such results as these attended the schism which agitated the fraternity of Free and Accepted Masons during the greater part of the eighteenth century. The jealousies which it excited, and the divisions and heart-burnings which it produced, have now subsided. Half a century of peaceful union has extinguished all that unappeasable hostility which marked its progress; and the historian may now venture on the details without incurring the hazard of exciting an angry feeling either in one party or the other, by faithfully unfolding the circumstances that gave rise to the secession, and attended its course till it was ultimately absorbed in the great body of English Freemasonry, at the re-union in 1813.

To make the subject intelligible, it will be

necessary to revert to the earliest times of Masonry in England. Passing over the Druids, and the Grand Mastership of St. Alban, which are unconnected with the question at issue, we find in an old Masonic manuscript the following important passage :—" Though the ancient records of the brotherhood in England were many of them destroyed or lost in the wars of the Saxons and Danes, yet King Athelstan, the grandson of King Alfred the Great, a mighty architect, the first anointed King of England, and who translated the Holy Bible into the Saxon tongue, A.D. 930, when he had brought the land into rest and peace, built many great works, and encouraged many Masons from France, who were appointed overseers thereof, and brought with them the charges and regulations of the Lodges, preserved since the Roman times; who also prevailed with the king to improve the constitution of the English lodges according to the foreign model. That the said king's brother, Prince Edwin, being taught Masonry, and taking upon him the charges of a Master Mason, for the love he had to the said craft, and the honourable principles whereon it is grounded, purchased a free charter of King Athelstan for the Masons; having a correction among themselves, as it was anciently expressed, or a freedom and power to regulate themselves, to amend what might happen amiss, *and to hold a yearly communication and general assembly.* That accordingly Prince Edwin *summoned all the Masons in the realm to meet him in a congregation at* YORK, who came and composed a general Lodge, of which he was Grand Master; and having brought with them all the writings and records extant, some in Greek, some in Latin, some in French, and other languages, from the contents thereof that assembly did frame the Constitutions and Charges of an English Lodge, and made a law to preserve and observe the same in all time coming."

From this document it is evident that Freemasonry in this island was first formally planted at York, which hence bears the same relation to English as Kilwinning does to Scottish Masonry, although its introduction into North Britain was two centuries later.[6]   A Grand Lodge was established at York, under the charter of Edwin, which maintained its functions, and asserted its supremacy down to the middle of the eighteenth

[6] It is probable that Masonry may have been introduced into Scotland about the same time as Christianity, although there are great objections to that theory; for in general the early buildings were not of stone, but of wood and wicker-work, and such as were of stone were extremely rude, and displayed no great knowledge of the Craft.   I am therefore disposed to think that scientific masonry, Freemasonry, or anything worthy of being dignified with the name of architecture, was not introduced into that country till the twelfth century.   But even although masonry may have been introduced at the same time as the Culdees, I cannot suppose that the Culdees were Freemasons; and great injury has been done to the Order by attributing to it much not only incapable of proof, but of which there are strong grounds for suspecting the reverse.   It appears to me that we have no proof of Freemasonry having existed in Scotland before the year 1126.

century. The name of an ancient York Mason was considered honourable in all ages; and the precedency has been conceded to it, by both the sister countries, as being of greater antiquity than the Kilwinning Masons of Scotland, or the Carrickfergus ones of Hibernia. There is no evidence of a general Grand Lodge being held in any other place during the whole of the above period, nor has its authority ever been made a subject of doubt or dispute. It is true its records have not been preserved, owing probably to the rash and mistaken zeal of some of its grand officers in 1720, who destroyed many of them, to prevent what they affected to consider an act of desecration.[7] But there is sufficient proof that its proceedings were uniform and regular, and the names of its Grand Masters are before us in the proper order of succession. And more than this, a MS. copy of the Constitutions of Athelstan, now in the British Museum, has been published by Mr. Halliwell, and its regulations are in perfect accordance with the Constitutions of Masonry at the present day.

During the reign of Queen Elizabeth, the government of the country attempted to interfere with its meetings, but without success. The

---

[7] Ware, in his Essay in the "Archæologia," says that Nicholas Stone destroyed many valuable papers belonging to the Society of Freemasons; and he adds, "Perhaps his master, Inigo Jones, thought that the new mode, though dependant on taste, was independent on science; and, like the calif Omar, that what was agreeable to the new faith was useless, and that what was not ought to be destroyed."

queen was jealous of all secrets in which she was unable to participate, and she deputed an armed force, on St. John's day, in December, 1561, to break up the annual Grand Lodge. The Grand Master, Sir Thomas Sackville, received the queen's officers with great civility, telling them that nothing would give him greater pleasure than to admit them into the Grand Lodge, and communicate to them the secrets of the Order. He persuaded them to be initiated, and this convinced them that the system was founded on the sublime ordinances of morality and religion. On their return, they assured the queen that the business of Freemasonry was the cultivation of morality and science, harmony and peace; and that politics and religion were alike forbidden to be discussed in their assemblies. The queen was perfectly satisfied, and never attempted to disturb them again.

The Fraternity was well governed by this Grand Lodge, which held its communications annually, and sometimes oftener; and the brethren at large were eligible to assemble in deliberation for the general benefit of the Craft. At these meetings the Grand Masters and Officers were installed, and other routine business transacted. This old Grand Lodge was the conservator of the primitive Gothic constitutions and charges; and under its benign patronage the works of art were executed which reflect such high credit on the Masons of the middle ages.

The establishment of a Grand Lodge in London

for the southern division of the island, in 1717, did not interfere with its proceedings; and the two Grand Lodges entertained a mutual good understanding towards each other for many years; until the more recent establishment grew powerful by the accession of noble and learned persons of the highest rank; who, being under the necessity of having a permanent town residence for the convenience of attending their parliamentary duties, found no difficulty in being regularly present at the quarterly Grand Lodges, and thus conveyed the influence of their talents and position in society to the southern division of the Order. Their example augmented the ranks of Masonry in the provinces, until the increase of its Lodges, both in numbers and respectability, in every part of England, was so rapid and uniform, that the Grand Lodge at York became inert, and at length silently resigned its authority into the hands of its more fortunate rival.

This appears to be a correct view of the case, because the Lodges in the City of York itself, as well as the entire north of England, have for many years practised the mysteries of the Craft under warrants granted by the London Grand Lodge; and are governed by Provincial Grand Masters of the same constitutional appointment.

The authority of the York Grand Lodge was not however superseded without a feeling of jealousy at the usurpations of its rival, which indiscreetly committed a few instances of aggression on its privileges that appear to be indefensible, as

the title of " Grand Lodge of *all* England " had
been conceded to it, while the London fraternity
assumed the appellation of " The Grand Lodge
of England." Taking advantage of an unfortunate dispute amongst the members of a Lodge at
York, the southern Grand Lodge encouraged the
seceding Brethren in their disobedience, by grant-
ing them a warrant to open a new Lodge under
its constitutions, in the city ; little dreaming how
soon a similar secession would occur in their own
body. This encroachment was not suffered to
pass without expostulation and protest on the
part of the ancient Grand Lodge, which contended that it would have been more in accordance with the genuine principles and regulations
of Masonry, if the refractory Brethren had been
admonished, and recommended to apply for readmission into the Lodge they had so inconsiderately abandoned.

This aggression having been attended with
success, was followed up in 1734, during the
Grand Mastership of the Earl of Crawford, by
the constitution of Lodges, the issue of deputa-
tions, and the appointment of Provincial Grand
Masters for Northumberland, Lancashire, and
Durham; all within the jurisdiction of the Grand
Lodge at York.[8] So direct an invasion of its

___

[8] Matthew Ridley, Esq., was appointed to the P. G. Mastership of Northumberland ; Edward Entwistle, Esq., to that of
Lancashire ; and Joseph Laycock, Esq., to that of Durham.
And the London Grand Lodge pronounced that all the Lodges
in those provinces were under its authority.

ancient rights was highly offensive; but the York Masons finding themselves too feeble to stem the torrent, after an ineffectual protest, held on their course in a dignified silence for a few years; and, although the rights of their Grand Lodge were superseded, and its influence weakened by the increasing prosperity of its rival, continued to act on their own independent authority, which was never called into question. Even after the dominion of the London Grand Lodge became indisputably established, and it considered itself entitled to the homage of the whole island south of the river Tweed, the one old Lodge at York was always excepted.[9]

[9] Thus it was resolved, during the Grand Mastership of the Earl of Carnarvon, afterwards Duke of Chandos, that "All Lodges are under the patronage of our Grand Master of England, except the old Lodge in York city, and the Lodges of Scotland, Ireland, France, and Italy, which, affecting independency, are under their own Grand Masters."—*Anderson's Const.* 1738, p. 196.

CHAPTER II.

THE EPITHETS "ANCIENT" AND "MODERN" EXPLAINED.

ABOUT the year 1737 or 1738, commenced that notable schism which again divided the English fraternity into two separate and independent sections, by the establishment of another Grand Lodge in London, and the appointment of a new Grand Master, with his staff of officers. It will be observed in limine, that, at this time, private Lodges did not possess the power of conferring either the second or third degree, which was a privilege reserved by the Grand Lodge for its own peculiar exercise; and these degrees were given as the reward of meritorious Brethren, who had rendered essential services to the Craft, either by their learning, talent, or activity; and this only with the unanimous consent of all the Brethren assembled in communication. An infringement of this privilege led to very serious and important consequences.

A few ambitious Brethren, who were ineligible for these degrees, prevailed on some inconsiderate Master Masons to open an illegal Lodge, and to pass, and raise them to the sublime degree.

These irregularities having escaped immediate detection, the same Brethren proceeded to initiate new members into the Order; and attempted to invest them with Masonic privileges. A project so bold and unprecedented could not elude ultimate discovery. The newly initiated Masons, proud of their acquisition, applied, in the character of visitors, for admission into the regular Lodges, when their pretensions were speedily unmasked, and the authors of the imposition were called on to vindicate their conduct before the Grand Lodge.[1] Complaints were preferred against them at the Quarterly Communication in June, 1739, and the offending Brethren were allowed six months to prepare their defence. After a full investigation and proof of their delinquency, it was resolved that "the transgressors should be pardoned upon their submission and promises of future good behaviour." It was also resolved, that "the laws shall be strictly put in execution against all Brethren who shall, in future, countenance, connive, or assist at any irregular makings."

The delinquents, though pardoned, appear to have been highly dissatisfied with this decision, which they affected to consider in the light of an indirect censure; and having tasted the sweets of their former illicit proceedings, they assumed the position of persecuted Brethren, and converted the resolutions of the Grand Lodge into a pretext

[1] MS. Penes me.

for persisting in their contumacy; and in open violation of the constitutions, they continued to meet as Masons in unauthorized places, to initiate, pass, and raise candidates, and to perform all the functions of a warranted Lodge, under the plea that in ancient times a sufficient number of Masons residing within a certain district, with the consent of the civil magistrate, were empowered to meet for the purpose of making Masons, and practising the rites of Masonry, without warrant of constitution; and that the privilege was inherent in themselves as individual Masons.

But the first meeting at the revival in 1717, under Anthony Sayer, Grand Master, had agreed, as a preliminary measure towards the formation of a Grand Lodge, and to cement its power, that this privilege should no longer exist. And it was unanimously resolved, that the privilege of assembling as Masons, which had been hitherto unrestricted, should be vested in certain Lodges or assemblies of Masons convened in certain places; and that every Lodge to be hereafter convened, except the four old Lodges at this time existing, should be legally authorized to act, by a warrant from the Grand Master for the time being, granted to certain individuals, by petition, with the consent and approbation of the Grand Lodge in communication; and that *without such warrant no Lodge should hereafter be deemed regular or constitutional.*"[2]

[2] "This regulation was found necessary," says a Continental writer, "because that here and there private Lodges were

The seceding Brethren contended that the above assembly did not possess the power to pass such a resolution, because it was not only self-created, but defective in numbers; whereas, "in order to form what Masons mean by a Grand Lodge, there should have been the Masters and Wardens of *five* regular Lodges, that is to say, five Masters and ten Wardens, making the number of installed officers fifteen. This is so well known to every man conversant with the ancient laws, usages, customs, and ceremonies of Master Masons, that it is needless to say more, than that the foundation was defective in number, and consequently defective in form and capacity." [3] And that, although they called the assembly a revival of the Grand Lodge, it was a gratuitous assumption which could not be verified by facts; because "had it been a revival of the ancient Craft only, without innovations or alterations of any kind, the Free and Accepted Masons in Ireland, Scotland, the East and West Indies, and America, where no change has yet happened, nay, Freemasons in general, would agree in secret language

formed by false and unworthy Brethren, who used a ritual of their own, and pretended to make men Freemasons, for the sake of their money. Some countries, particularly Denmark and Prussia, have passed laws that no Lodge shall be held or formed in any part of their dominions without having first obtained a warrant from one of the Grand Lodges. In Germany, there are a few of the ancient Lodges which are independent, and which have not joined any Grand Lodge, but which, on account of their age, are acknowledged as regular Lodges by all the others."

[3] Ahiman Rezon, p. viii. Ed. 1813.

and ceremonies with the members of the *modern* Lodges. But daily experience points out the contrary; and this is an incontrovertible proof of the falsehood of the supposed revival." [4]

These arguments and reflections, however, were unheeded by the Grand Lodge, or considered as serving only to aggravate the offence: and stringent resolutions were passed to check their proceedings, which produced only a temporary effect; for several Lodges having been erased from the lists for refusing to attend the Grand Master in Quarterly Communication, pursuant to notices repeatedly served on them for that purpose, the members united themselves with the seceders, and succeeding in forming a body of sufficient strength to cast off their allegiance openly to the metropolitan Grand Lodge. As there had been, before this period, some differences between the Grand Lodges of London and York, the schismatics assumed the name and authority of the latter, although it is doubtful whether that body gave any sanction to their illegal proceedings. Laurie [5] asserts that the sanction was only " pretended;" and Noorthouck positively says, that they had no encouragement whatever from the Grand Lodge at York. His words are—" Under a fictitious sanction of the ancient York constitution, which was dropped at the revival of the Grand Lodge in 1717, they presumed to claim the right of constituting Lodges. Some Brethren at York con-

---

[4] Ahiman Rezon, p. ix.　　　　　[5] Page 116.

tinued, indeed, to act under their original constitution; *but the irregular Masons in London never
received any patronage from them.*" [6]

The constitutional Grand Lodge now took the
matter into its most serious consideration, and
attempted to bring the refractory Brethren to a
proper sense of duty, that they might return to
their allegiance, and be received with affection
and forgiveness. Failing in this endeavour, it
resolved at length to adopt the expedient, appa-
rently rendered necessary by the emergency, but
extremely ill-judged, of introducing a slight alteration into the system, which might have the effect
of detecting the schismatics, and thus excluding
them from the orthodox Lodges.[7] The resolution was unfortunate, and produced the very evil
which it was intended to avert.

The Grand Lodge now expressly ordered the
regular Lodges not to admit the seceding Brethren
as visitors, or to countenance or acknowledge
them in any way whatever, but to treat them as

[6] Const. p. 240.

[7] This alteration is thus explained by a cotemporary writer :
—"I would beg leave to ask whether two persons standing in
the Guildhall of London, the one facing the statues of Gog and
Magog, and the other with his back turned on them, could,
with any degree of propriety, quarrel about their situation, as
Gog must be on the right of one, and Magog on the right of
the other ? Such, and far more insignificant, is the disputatious
temper of the seceding Brethren, that, on no better grounds
than the above, they chose to usurp a power, and to act in open
and direct violation of the regulations they had solemnly engaged
to maintain, and by every artifice possible to be devised, endeavoured to increase their numbers."

persons unworthy of notice, until they humbled themselves as the Grand Master shall in his prudence direct, and until he signifies his approval by a missive directed to the regular Lodges. The Grand Lodge further recommended the utmost care and circumspection in the examination of visitors; and not to admit them on any pretence whatever, until they had entered into an engagement that they had been regularly initiated, passed, and raised, in a lawful, warranted Lodge.

These regulations were a source of exultation and triumph to the seceding Brethren. They loudly exclaimed against what they termed an alteration of the landmarks, as an unprecedented and unconstitutional proceeding; accused the Grand Lodge of having deviated from ancient usage, and conferred upon all its members and adherents the invidious epithet of *modern* Masons,[8] while they appropriated to themselves the exclusive and honourable title of "*ancient* Masons, acting under the old York constitutions, cemented

[8] The offence was increased by the manner in which they recorded their opinions on this invidious subject. They charged the Grand Lodge with a design of abolishing the old custom of explaining geometry in the Lodges, and substituting conviviality in its stead. "Some of the young Brethren," they said, "made it appear that a good knife and fork in the hands of a dexterous Brother over proper materials, would give greater satisfaction, and add more to the conviviality of the Lodge, than the best scale and compasses in Europe." They further asserted that the Brethren had made an attempt to get rid of their aprons, because "they made the gentlemen look like mechanics." —*Ahiman Rezon*, p. 14.

and consecrated by immemorial observance."
Taking advantage of this popular cry, they proceeded to the formation of an independent Grand
Lodge, drew up a code of laws for its government,
issued warrants for the constitution of new Lodges,
"under the true ancient system of Freemasonry;"
and from the fees arising out of these proceedings
they succeeded in establishing a fund of benevolence, besides defraying the current expenses of
the institution.

CHAPTER III.

ORIGIN OF THE ROYAL ARCH.

IT will be necessary to pause a moment here for the purpose of taking into consideration a few anomalies in this new establishment, which appear difficult of solution. The *ancients*,[1] in their justification, had strongly and repeatedly condemned the formation of any new Grand Lodge, as an unconstitutional proceeding, and at variance with the genuine principles of Masonry; and pronounced that such a body, being self-constituted, could not possess any legal authority over the Craft. But if they were sincere in their protestations, why did they constitute a Grand Lodge of their own? And again, if they really derived their authority from the Grand Lodge at York, why did they not unite under its banner, refer to it for their warrants and other public sanctions, instead of openly renouncing its protection by the establishment of a new Grand Lodge, and

---

[1] I shall use the words *ancients* and *moderns* in their general acceptation; the former to designate the seceders, and the latter the constitutional Masons; although both were alike either ancient or modern, being equally derived from the same source.'

issuing constitutions for the formation of private
Lodges, even in the city of York itself? These
queries are difficult to answer, and therefore the
ancients wisely avoided them. Not a word on
the subject is to be found in the Ahiman Rezon,
though, as we have already seen, it is sufficiently
vituperative on other points.[2]

The accusation of changing the ancient landmarks of the Order, which was pertinaciously
urged against the Grand Lodge of the moderns,
answered every purpose which was intended to
be effected by it. The new Order became
extremely popular, and as it professed to convey
privileges, and to communicate secrets unknown
to the rival institution, persons of rank were
induced to enrol themselves under its banner.

But, notwithstanding the virtuous indignation
which was expressed by the ancients at the alleged
delinquency of the English Grand Lodge, I am
inclined to think that they themselves, at the
above period, remodified, at the least, if they did
not alter, several of the old landmarks. It was
asserted by Finch, and some other Masonic char-
latans, that the Master Mason's word was never
lost! And although, when this public announce-

---

[2] Laurie says of this book :—" The unfairness with which he
(Dermott) has stated the proceedings of the moderns, the
bitterness with which he treats them, and the quackery and
vain glory with which he displays his own pretensions to
superior knowledge, deserve to be reprobated by every class of
Masons who are anxious for the purity of their Order, and the
preservation of that charity and mildness which ought to
characterize all their proceedings."—Laurie, p. 117.

ment was made, it was considered merely as an ingenious fiction to attract attention to their worthless publications; yet there is circumstantial evidence, which may induce us to suspend our opinions on the truth or falsehood of the assertion. These considerations afford a clue towards discovering the origin of the English Royal Arch order, which, I think, it would be difficult to trace beyond the period of this schism, although I admit the imperfection of written evidence in proof of facts attached to a secret society, which professes to transmit its peculiar mysteries by oral communication only.

Sir William Drummond, the erudite author of the Origines, has recorded the opinion that " it is painful to have doubts where others believe; " and I myself have long felt the force of this sentiment with respect to the Royal Arch. At my first exaltation in 1813, I was taught to believe it an ancient degree; but I confess, that even at that early period I entertained considerable doubts on the point. The degree is too incongruous to be of any great antiquity. It exhibits too many evidences of modern construction to be received with implicit credence as a ceremony practised by the ancient Dionysiacs, or even the more modern colleges of Freemasons, or confraternities of the middle ages, to whom we are indebted for the sublime specimens of science and genius exhibited in the ecclesiastical buildings, which still dignify and adorn every European nation. It is not mentioned in any ancient record of acknowledged authenticity; nor does Dr. Anderson give the slightest hint, in his elaborate history of the Order, that it was known at the period when he wrote.

The earliest mention of it in England which I can find is in the year 1740, just one year after the trifling alteration sanctioned by the modern Grand Lodge already mentioned. An old Master Mason's tracing-board or floor-cloth, published on the Continent almost immediately after symbolical Masonry had been received in France as a branch from the Grand Lodge in England in 1725, which furnished the French Masons with a written copy of the lectures then in use, contains the true Master's word in a very prominent situation.[3] This forms an important link in the chain of presumptive evidence, that the word, at that time, had not been severed from the third degree and transferred to another. If this be true, as there is every reason to believe, the alteration must have been effected by some extraordinary innovation and change of landmarks. And I am persuaded, for reasons which will speedily be given, that the seceding Brethren are chargeable with originating these innovations; for the division of the third degree and the fabrication of the English Royal Arch appear, on their own showing, to have been their work.

Now their Master Mason's degree, which included, as we shall see, the germs of our present

---

[3] MS. penes me.

Royal Arch, although it contained elements of the greatest sublimity, was imperfect in its construction, and unsatisfactory in its result; which will tend to show, from the crude and unfinished state in which it then appeared, that the degree was in its infancy. The anachronisms with which it·abounded, and the loose manner in which its parts were fitted into each other, betrayed its recent origin. In fact, it was evidently an attempt to combine several of the continental degrees of sublime Masonry into one, without regard to the order of time, propriety of arrangement, or any other consistent principle ; and therefore we find, in the degree as it was originally constructed, jumbled together in a state of inextricable confusion, certain detailed events commemorated in Ramsay's Royal Arch, the Knights of the Ninth Arch, and many others, particularly the Rite called the Ancien de Bouillon, which was the real name of the degree, and it was on this authority that they denominated themselves Ancient Masons. It is impossible to be explicit on this part of the subject, because the particulars cannot legally be committed to writing ; nor is it material, for it is the origin and not the details of the Royal Arch that I am now principally concerned to show. The fabricators might—it is barely possible—have had *the idea* from the sister island, but they could not have imported the degree from thence, because, if practised by the Irish Masons at that period (which is extremely doubtful), it was altogether a different composition.

c 2

CHAPTER IV.

SPURIOUS DEGREES.

I PROCEED to show the presumption that the Royal Arch degree was concocted by the ancients to widen the breach, and make the line of distinction between them broader and more indelible. Colonel Stone says, " It is asserted, but with how much truth I have not the means of deciding, that the first warrant for the practice of the Royal Arch degree was granted by Charles Edward Stuart, son of the Pretender, to hold a Chapter of an order called the Scotch Jacobite, at Arras, in France, where he had received many favours at the hands of the Masons. This Chapter was subsequently removed to Paris, where it was called Le Chapitre d'Arras, *and is, in fact, the original of our present Royal Arch Chapters.*" Stone's information on the foreign degrees, however, was very imperfect; for there is no evidence to prove that the English Royal Arch was ever worked in France. The Chapter established under the auspices of the Chevalier was denominated the Eagle and Pelican,[1] another name for

[1] It is wonderful to reflect on the number of spurious Masonic degrees which had the Eagle for their symbol !—As,

the Royal Order of Bruce, or that part of it which is called the R.S.Y.C.S., a composition of a widely different nature from our Royal Arch.

In compiling the Ahiman Rezon, Dermott was particularly guarded lest he should make any undue disclosures which might betray the English origin of his degree, for it would have destroyed his claim to the title of an *ancient* Mason; but, notwithstanding all his care, I shall be able to prove the fact almost from the Ahiman Rezon itself, with the assistance of a little analogous testimony collected from other sources. It was evidently his intention that the Royal Arch should be received amongst the Brethren as a foreign degree, which had been practised from the most ancient times. Now it could not be a continental rite, because it does not correspond with the Royal Arch propagated by Ramsay on the continent of Europe; neither is it found in any of the French or German systems of Masonry practised during the early part or middle of the last century. It is not contained in the Royal Order of Bruce, which is the only ancient system of Masonry in existence, except the three blue

for instance, Chevalier de l'Aigle, ou des Maîtres élus ; Chevalier de l'Aigle, ou le Maître parfait en Architecture ; Chevalier de l'Aigle et du Pélican ; Chevalier de l'Aigle blanc et noir ; Illustre Chevalier Commandeur de l'Aigle blanc et noir ; Chevalier de l'Aigle noir ; Le Prince de l'Aigle noir ; Le Prince du Grand Aigle noir ; Chevalier de l'Aigle d'Or ; Chevalier de l'Aigle Prussien ; Chevalier de l'Aigle renversé ; Chevalier de l'Aigle rouge ; Ordre des deux Aigles ; Chevalier des deux Aigles couronnés ; Ancien et accepté, &c., &c., &c.

degrees; neither do we discover it in the systems
of Charles Edward Stuart, of the Chapter of
Clermont, in the degrees of Baron Hunde, in
Hermetic, Cabalistic, or Eclectic Masonry; nor
in the elaborate rites of Zinnendorff, Swedenborg,
Fessler, Bedaridde, Peuvret, or their compeers.
It was not included in the order of Mizraim, Adop-
tive Masonry, or the Rite Ancien et Accepté; nor,
I am persuaded, in any other system which was
ever practised on the continent of Europe. If it
were, I have failed in my endeavours to discover it.
It is therefore very properly denominated the
English Royal Arch, for it was doubtless a fabrication of this country, and from hence was transmitted to every part of the world where it now
prevails. Let us then endeavour to ascertain its
precise origin.

The ancients proclaimed to the public in their
Book of Constitutions—" It is a truth beyond
contradiction, the Free and Accepted Masons in
Ireland and Scotland, and the ancient Masons of
England, have one and the same customs, usages,
and ceremonies; but this is not the case with the
modern Masons in England, *who differ materially*,
not only from the above, but from most Masons
in all parts of the world."[2] And in another
place they state particularly what some of these
points of difference were, viz., " they differ exceedingly in *makings, ceremonies, knowledge, Masonic
language, and installations;* so much so that they

---

[2] Ahiman Rezon, p. 70.

always have been, and still continue to be, two distinct societies, totally independent of each other." [3] To authorize such assertions as these there must have been some organic difference, which could be nothing short of the institution of a new degree, practised in the ancient Lodges. And to make it the more attractive, they dignified it with the title of the Royal Arch, or Rite de Bouillon, as Ramsay had done before them, although their degree differed materially from that which he had promulgated under the same name. It is, however, extremely probable that Ramsay may have had some hand in this business; for he visited London at the very period in question, for the purpose of introducing his new degrees into English Masonry; and his schemes being rejected by the constitutional Grand Lodge, nothing appears more likely than that he would throw himself into the hands of the schismatics, who would receive his communications with pleasure, because they presented the means of furthering their views in the propagation of what they termed ancient Masonry. And under these circumstances a new degree, or rather new ceremonies, were concocted, [4] which promised to cement

---

[3] Abiman Rezon, p. 30.

[4] In the R. A. of Ramsay there was a jewel inscribed with the letters I. V. I. O. L., meaning Inveni verbum in ore Leonis, of which the following explanation was given in the historical lecture attached to the degree:— "Biblical history informs us that the Jews were slaves to the Egyptians until they were redeemed by Moses, for the purpose of occupying the promised land. We also learn from the annals deposited in the archives

the schism, and prove an effectual bar to all reconciliation, by constituting a tangible line of demar-
cation between them and the moderns, which
would be impregnable. Dermott confesses that
the Royal Arch WAS FIRST PRACTISED in England
by "the Excellent Masons of the Grand Lodge of
England *according to the old constitutions*, who,

in Scotland (?), and only to be examined by us, that in a certain
battle the ark of alliance was lost in a forest, and was subsequently
found by the roaring of a lion, which, on the approach of the
Israelites, ceased its roarings, and couched at their feet. This
lion had previously devoured a great number of the Egyptians
who attempted to carry away the ark, keeping securely in his
mouth the key to the treasures which it contained. But when
the high priest came near him, he dropped the key from his
mouth, and retired couching and tame, without offering the
least violence to the chosen people." There is a similar allusion
to a lion in the degree of the venerable Grand Master of all
Symbolic Lodges, or Master ad vitam, where he is represented
as having been wounded by an arrow, and having escaped from
the stake to which he had been bound, lay at the mouth of a
cave with the broken rope about his neck, using certain mathematical instruments. At the foot of the stake lay a crown.
This bore a reference to the escape of Charles Edward Stuart,
the claimant to the crown of England ; and in the lectures a
question is asked, "What does Jackson signify ?" which is thus
answered :—"I am that I am, which is the name of him who
found the cavern where the lion was hid that kept in his mouth
the key of the ark of alliance, which was lost, as is mentioned in
the degree of the R. A." It is now universally allowed that
Jackson means Jaques-son, the son of James, the exiled king.
There can be no doubt but Ramsay invented the French Royal
Arch, and made it the highest of all his degrees, and the *ne plus
ultra* of Masonry. The fact is, the above was a symbol to signify
the lion of the tribe of Judah, or Christ, pierced with the spear,
and bearing the key to unlock and explain the tendency of the
Jewish dispensation, and its reference to Christianity.

duly assembled, and constitutionally convened in general Grand Chapter, carefully collected and revised the regulations *which have long been in use* for the government thereof;" [5] thus asserting their claim to antiquity, although it had never yet been practised in England. Ramsay had already made the same claim for the antiquity of his degrees, which, it is well known, were invented by himself. It is, therefore, extremely probable that Ramsay was concerned in the fabrication of the English degree; because it still embodies some of the details of his Royal Arch, the whole of which, I am inclined to think, in the earliest arrangement of the English degree formed one of the preliminary ceremonies.[6]

[5] Laws and Regulations of the Holy Royal Arch in the "Ahiman Rezon," p. 114.

[6] I make this statement, because the earliest copy of this degree in my possession, dated 1788, commences with a long explanation of the ceremonies of Ramsay's Royal Arch as preparatory to the English degree. This ceremonial had been discontinued before my own exaltation in 1813; and probably not long before; because a copy of the lectures, which was placed in my hands by a friend at that period, opens with the details of Enoch's arches; but this portion had been obliterated by running a pen through it. The notorious Masonic quack, Finch, in the explanation of one of his engravings, says "the four equilateral triangles within the perpendicular part is emblematic of the *Suspended Arch, Advanced Arch, Dedicated Arch, and Circumscribed Arch;* and the twelve letters are the initials of the proper words belonging to these four points of the Royal Arch degree. In the right-hand corner is *another Cross relative to the Royal Arch, with nine perpendicular Arches, made by Enoch, and discovered by Solomon.* The Z stands for the chief officer of the Chapter, and the equilateral triangle round the

Besides, Dermott could not have derived his degree from any other source, for the age of continental innovation had only just commenced, and Ramsay's degrees were the only new introductions grafted upon symbolical Masonry in France. The Freemasonry which was practised in that country, between A.D. 1700 and 1725, was only by some English residents, without a charter or any formal Lodge. The first warrant for opening a Lodge in France, was granted in 1725, by the Grand Lodge of England to Lord Derwentwater, Maskelyne, Higuetty, and some other French followers of the Pretender, who met at an eating-house in the Rue des Boucheries. It was not till 1728 that Ramsay added his new degrees; and this gave the idea of the hauts grades, which soon came into vogue; but they were received with suspicion, and made little progress for some years.[7] In December, 1736, Lord Harnouester was elected

letter Z alludes to the triangular chains of the Jews during part of their Babylonish captivity." The real ceremonies of this surreptitious third Degree were, however, essentially different from Ramsay's Royal Arch, as will be shown in a subsequent chapter.

[7] We have the testimony of Professor Robison, the anti-Mason, that "Ramsay was as eminent for his piety as he was for his enthusiasm, but his opinions were singular. His eminent learning, his elegant talents, his amiable character, and particularly his estimation at court, gave great influence to everything he said on the subject of Masonry, which was merely a matter of fashion and amusement. Whoever has attended much to human affairs knows *the eagerness with which men propagate all singular opinions, and the delight which attends their favourable reception.*"

Grand Master for France, and Ramsay was installed into the office of Grand Orator. In 1740 he came over to England, and remained in this country more than a year; after which he returned to France, where the rage for innovation had now fairly commenced.

CHAPTER V.

THE MASTER'S PART.

It was during this period, I am persuaded, that the English Royal Arch was fabricated; for very soon afterwards the ancients publicly announced that "Ancient Masonry consists of *four* degrees," while modern Masonry had only three; the fourth signifying the Royal Arch, of which, until a much later period, the constitutional Grand Lodge professed to know nothing, but which was authoritatively pronounced by the ancients to be "an essential and component part of ancient Masonry, and that which is the perfection and end of the beautiful system." [1] The words of the preamble to the original laws of their Royal Arch, are these,—"Ancient Masonry consists of four degrees; the three first of which are those of the Apprentice, the Fellow-craft, and the sublime degree of Master; and a Brother, being well versed in these degrees, and otherwise qualified as hereafter will be expressed, is eligible to be admitted to the fourth degree, the Holy Royal Arch. *This degree is certainly more august, sublime, and important than*

[1] Ahiman Rezon, pp. 113, 114.

those which precede it, and is the summit and per-
fection of ancient Masonry. It impresses on our
minds a more firm belief of the existence of a
Supreme Deity, without beginning of days, or end
of years, and justly reminds us of the respect and
veneration due to that Holy Name. Until within
these few years, this degree was not conferred on
any but those who had been a considerable time
enrolled in the Fraternity; and could, besides,
give the most unequivocal proofs of their skill and
proficiency in the Craft." [2] In fact, until within
a few years before these laws were drawn up, it
was not conferred at all; for it was unknown.

In proof that the members of the constitutional
Grand Lodge were, at this period, ignorant of its
existence, and disclaimed its authority as a
Masonic innovation, the Grand Secretary of the
moderns stated, in answer to the petition of an
ancient Mason for pecuniary relief, about the year
1758—"Being an ancient Mason, you are not
entitled to any of our charity. The ancient
Masons have a Lodge at the 'Five Bells,' in the
Strand, and their secretary's name is Dermott.
OUR SOCIETY IS NEITHER ARCH, ROYAL ARCH,
nor ancient, so that you have no right to partake
of our charity." [3] It is clear, therefore, that the
moderns had no Royal Arch in 1758; and equally
clear that it had been long practised by the
ancients, who were entirely ignorant of it at the

---

[2] Ahiman Rezon, p. 113.

[3] A copy of this curious document will be found in the
" Ahiman Rezon." Introduction, p. xi.

first breaking out of the schism; for they were
then members of Lodges under the constitutions
of England; and if they were acquainted with
the degree, they were bound on their allegiance
to communicate it to their superiors, if, as they
afterwards asserted, it formed a constituent part
of ancient Masonry, which they did not do. And
if they were not acquainted with it, as it is reasonable to presume, how did they know it after the
schism, if it was not a new invention or a new communication? And it could not be the latter for
the reasons already stated. The conclusion is,
therefore, inevitable, that the ancients fabricated
the degree.

In confirmation of this fact, the same book of
constitutions declares, that "it is impossible to
exalt a modern Mason to the Royal Arch, without
previously conferring upon him the Master's
degree *according to their own ceremonies.*" [4] This
assertion was doubtlessly made on the ground that
he was already in possession of the Master's word,
which they knew was communicated in the third
degree, according to the terms of the " Master's
part," as then practised by the modern Grand
Lodge: for the first lectures which were drawn
up by Brothers Payne, Anderson, Desaguliers,
Martin Folks, Madden, and other eminent
Masons, expressly declare, in the degree of Master
that "that which was lost," meaning the Master
Mason's word, "*is now found;*" *i.e.* in the latter

---

[4] Ahiman Rezon,   20.

ceremonies of the third degree, when it was delivered to the newly-raised Master in due form; and, therefore, the Royal Arch degree would have thrown no new light on the subject to a constitutional Master Mason."[5]

This is a convincing proof that the difference between the ancient and modern systems consisted solely in the mutilation and extension of the third degree; and it is actually referred to in the proceedings of the modern Grand Lodge in 1755, where they express their disapprobation at the conduct of the ancients in "introducing *novelties and conceits of opinionative persons*, to created belief that there have been other societies of Masons *more ancient than this society;*"[6] evidently alluding to the establishment of the Royal Arch; which they publicly repudiated three years afterwards, as I have already shown, by declaring that they knew nothing of "either Arch or Royal Arch."

---

[5] A highly valued correspondent says, "Since I last wrote to you, I have had occasion to study much Masonry, both as to the history and origin of the several degrees, and its distinction into speculative and operative; and after the closest attention I can pay to the subject, I have come to the conclusion that no degrees are ancient except the three first. The R. A. degrees may or may not; but I cannot trace them much, if at all, beyond the middle of the last century: in fact, I have great doubts if they be not a modern compilation (I speak particularly of the R. A. degree itself); the idea having been taken from Ezekiel's vision, in the same way as the almost blasphemous foreign degree of the ———— is taken from the first chapter of Revelations."

[6] Noorthouck's Constitutions, p. 264.

These declarations appear to have created a
sensation amongst the Fraternity, which was
unfavourable to the seceders; and, therefore,
Dermott proceeded, in his own justification, to
charge the regular Grand Lodge with having concocted a new third degree at its first establishment, because the Masons who formed it were
ignorant of the Master's part. He says that
"About the year 1717, some joyous companions
who had passed the degree of a Craft, though
very rusty, resolved to form a Lodge for themselves, in order, by conversation, to recollect what
had formerly been dictated to them; or if that
should be found impracticable, *to substitute something new, which might for the future pass for
Masonry among themselves.* At this meeting the
question was asked, whether any person in the
assembly knew the Master's part; and being
answered in the negative, it was resolved that *the
deficiency should be made up with a new composition,* and what fragments of the old Order could
be found among them, should be immediately
re-formed, and made more pliable to the humours
of the people." [7]   It will be needless to add that
this is an exaggeration; because it is very im-
probable that the Brethren who were acting in
the four old Lodges in existence at that period,
with Sayer, Payne, Lamball, Capt. Elliott, and
other eminent Brethren at their head, should be
ignorant of the ceremonies of the third degree.

Ahiman Rezon, p. 23.

From the above facts and arguments we may rationally conclude that the Royal Arch was practised at that period by the ancient Masons only.[8]

[8] At the fabrication of this degree, it is evident that the word "Keystone" was used; for Dermott, who was doubtless the individual to whom its origin may, in a great measure, be attributed, in an epilogue of his composition, which was spoken at the Theatre Royal at the Haymarket, has the following passage, in evident allusion to it :—

> "The men, too, can build, as their fancy best suits,
>   With curls on each side like a pair of volutes ;
>   High toupees in front, something like a KEYSTONE," &c.

I think he was right in the use of this word, which certainly was used originally. In Dunckerley's Ritual it is thus exemplified. "What do we three represent in the chapter ? The Three Keystones which all must draw before they can obtain the M. G. and S. W." Our Supreme Grand Chapter has substituted the words "cape stone," to imply that the subterranean passage of those early ages was not vaulted, but covered with a flat stone roof supported by pillars, after the manner of the Egyptian temples ; under an impression, I suppose, that arches and keystones were unknown at the building of Solomon's Temple. The subject is of sufficient importance to merit a brief examination, because modern discovery has confirmed the belief that the use of the keystone is older than the first temple. Mr. King, indeed, asserts that "arches were not used for a thousand years after the building of King Solomon's Temple ;" and as a proof of it, he cites the temples of Zerubbabel and Herod, which contained no arches ; nor are they mentioned by Homer. None, he says, were introduced into the magnificent buildings either of Babylon or Persepolis ; neither were they made use of at Athens ; in the temple of Diana at Ephesus ; nor in Egypt, except in the edifices which were constructed after the time of the Ptolemies ; and he concludes by assigning the honour of the invention to Archimedes.—(Mun. Antiq., vol. ii., p. 225.) But subsequent investigations have shown the

It appears further that the degree was then conferred, in the Master's Lodge; for separate chapters were a subsequent introduction, as also was the change of colour.   The records state, that " every regular and warranted Lodge possesses the power of forming and holding meetings in each of these several degrees, the last of which, from its pre-eminence, it is denominated a chapter."9 But these regulations were drawn up many years after the first establishment of the R.A.

inaccuracy of this opinion.   It is now clear that the arch and keystone were known to the Tyrians before the time of Solomon.   "An opinion," says Mr. Wilkinson, in his Topography of Thebes, "admitted by the generality of the learned world, gains force by want of contradiction, till at length it passes into fact.   The arch was employed in the houses of the Egyptians, owing to the small quantity of wood growing in the country, and in roofing the chambers of the crude brick pyramids.   I had long been persuaded that the greater part of the brick vaults in the western tombs of Thebes were at least coeval with the eighteenth dynasty, but had never been fortunate enough to find proofs in support of my conjecture, till chance threw in my way a tomb, vaulted in the usual manner, *with an arched doorway* of the same materials, stuccoed, and bearing in every part of the fresco paintings, the name of Amenoph I.   Innumerable vaults and arches exist at Thebes, of early date, but unfortunately none with the names of kings remaining on them.   *The above discovery carries the existence of the arch up to B. C.* 1540, *or* 450 *years before the building of King Solomon's Temple.*"   And the same Egyptian antiquary thinks that they were known at a still earlier period.   Dr. Clarke carries arches up to the time of Abraham, an opinion which is corroborated by Sir W. Gell.— *Argolis*, p. 56.

9 Ahiman Rezon, p. 14.

CHAPTER VI.

THE DEGREE OF GEOMETRICAL MASTER.

THE seceding Masons who met at the Ben Jonson's Lodge, in Spital Fields, styled their exalted Brethren "Excellent Masons," which is another proof that the degree had been adapted from Continental Masonry, and that the fabricators were desirous of inculcating the belief that it was a foreign rite. This is further confirmed by what the "Ahiman Rezon" says of the Lodge at the "Ben Jonson's Head," that "Some of the Brethren *had been abroad*, and received extraordinary benefits on account of ancient Masonry."[1] The excellent Masons were alone eligible to be present during an exaltation. It is evident that Dermott knew nothing of *the degree so called*, which is a more modern compilation, because if he had, his R.A. or Ne plus ultra would have constituted a fifth degree, and this was repudiated by his preliminary announcement that "Freemasonry contains *four* degrees, and no more." The name of *Excellent* was, therefore,

[1] Ahiman Rezon, p. 12.

a mere distinction applied to those who had received the new degree. And this argument will serve to prove that the Past Master's was also unknown *as a degree*, it being then considered as a simple ceremony, and was confined to those who had actually occupied the chair of their Lodge.

When the General Grand Chapter was formed, the degree was dignified with the name of *Most Excellent ;* the chief officers of the Grand Lodge were considered *ex officio* as " Grand Chiefs " of the Royal Arch; and in the end warrants were pronounced necessary to authorize Lodges to confer the degree; and the fee was stated at one guinea. These, however, appear to have been gradual steps; and many years elapsed before the system was arranged, and the Order of the Royal Arch organized so as to constitute an independent rite. Altogether it was a bold proceeding; but Bro. Dermott was an intrepid character; [2] and he succeeded in establishing quietly in England that which excited on the continent of Europe opposition and tumult, and sometimes exposure and disgrace.

It is true, the degree was unattended with any

[2] Sir W. Drummond (" Origines," vol. i., p. 13), speaking of the fabulous history of the Chaldeans, says,—" Mankind are seldom satisfied with remaining in doubt, when conjecture can explain what curiosity desires to know. The bold invent, and the credulous believe. Imagination embellishes tradition, illumines the dark pages of history, and builds on the early and doubtful annals of former times some glittering edifice, which dazzles the eyes of the ignorant, and which even pleases the spectator who doubts of its solidity."

speculative doctrines of a questionable or dangerous nature; and, therefore, it was not likely to excite an extraordinary degree of attention in the recipients. It embodied none of those theosophic notions which pervaded some of the Teutonic systems of continental Masonry; it promulgated no doctrines which were prejudicial to the interests of morality; and for these reasons it escaped animadversion. It aimed to embody the sublimities of religion, and to hallow the attributes of the Most High. And while it pointed to the prophecy of Jacob, that "the sceptre should not depart from Judah until Shiloh come,"[3] the prejudices of the Christian and the Jew would be alike conciliated, and no one would feel justified in questioning the propriety of an extension of the third degree, while its object was reputed to promote the glory of God, peace on earth, and good-will amongst mankind.

Even after the Grand Chapter was formed, it was only necessary to produce a certificate that the applicant was "a Geometrical Master Mason" to entitle him to be *passed*[4] to the Royal Arch; and the candidate was privately *passed the chair* as a preliminary ceremony;[5] a custom that was

---

[3] The name given to the Chapter No. 1 of the modern system, viz., "The Rock and Fountain Shiloh," is a proof that our Brethren of that age considered the Royal Arch to be a Christian degree; for the above title interprets Shiloh as Christ, and refers to the fountain of his blood springing from the rock of our salvation.

[4] This is the word that was then used.

[5] The qualifications of a candidate at that period, as I find by

used till the Union, in 1813.[6] This extension of
the primitive principles of the Order was subsequently adopted by the constitutional Masons
under the Grand Lodge of England, who remo-

an old MS. in my possession, were these :—"Brethren who had
distinguished themselves in Craft Masonry, not only by their
learning and talent, but by their love of Masonry, their activity,
generosity, and liberality of sentiment. They must have shown
themselves possessed of a great desire to increase their Masonic
knowledge, and to promote the general interests of the society ;
not governed by either enthusiasm or bigotry, but by a general
love to the human race. They cannot be admitted until they
have passed through the degrees of Craft Masonry, nor until
they have attained the age of twenty-five years, unless their
father be a Companion of the sublime degree, and then they
may be admitted, if well recommended, balloted for, and
approved, at three several periods, at the age of twenty-three."

[6] The fact is proved by the form of the official documents.
Before the degree was conferred, the following certificate was
issued by the Master and Wardens :—"Whereas our trusty
and well-beloved Brother ————, a Geometrical Master
Mason, and member of our Lodge, has solicited us to recommend him as *a Master Mason*, every way qualified for passing
the Holy Royal Arch ; we do hereby certify that, so far as we
are judges of the necessary qualifications, the said Brother has
obtained the unanimous consent of our Lodge for this recom-
mendation." But after the candidate had received the degree,
this certificate was issued to authorize his registration in the
books of the Grand Chapter :—"We, the three Chiefs and
Scribe, whose names are hereunto subscribed, do certify, that
in a Chapter of Holy Royal Arch, convened and held under
the sanction and authority of the worshipful Lodge No. —, our
beloved Brother ————, having delivered to us the recom-
mendation of the Lodge ————, hereunto subjoined, and
proved himself, by due examination, to be well qualified in the
several degrees of Apprentice, Fellowcraft, and Master Mason,
and having passed the chair, was by us admitted to the supreme
degree of Excellent R. A. Mason."

delled the degree, and brought it to its present form after many judicious alterations and improvements; but the period when it was first introduced amongst them is uncertain. The edition of Preston's Illustrations, dated 1781, contains no reference whatever to the Royal Arch; but in the very next edition, after the author had been admitted into the Fraternity of the ancients, the word "Companion" occurs in reference to the Grand Chapter of Harodim, established by the constitutional Grand Lodge in 1787, which, says he, "for some years was faintly encouraged; but after its merit had been further investigated, it received the patronage of several exalted Masonic characters." The poetical department of the first-named edition contains no Arch songs, while the latter contains several. Bro. Dunckerley composed his Royal Arch songs between these two dates. The introduction of the Royal Arch degree into the modern system could not, therefore, be earlier than the dedication of Freemasons' Hall in 1776. Ten years after this date, the regulations of the degree were first published. I have before me a list of the Grand Officers in 1788, which shows the state of the Royal Arch at that period; and from the number of Past Grand Masters Z, which was then an annual office, being only eight, the presumption is that the Grand Chapter had been formed only eight or nine years previously—viz., in 1779.[7] But it was not till

---

[7] The names of these eight were Comps. James Galloway, Esq.; Thomas Dunckerley, Esq.; John Brooks, Esq.; James

the year 1785 that newly exalted Companions were required to pay a registration fee.

At the period of its introduction by the ancients, however, and before the moderns ever contemplated its use amongst themselves, the Grand Lodge was alarmed at the innovation; and when the Marquis of Caernarvon was elected to the office of Grand Master, he applied himself steadily to the extinction of the schism. His acting deputy, Dr. Manningham, conducted the proceedings, and pointed out the necessity of discouraging such an open violation of the laws of the society, by some decisive measures. At a Grand Lodge holden on the 20th of March, 1755, a formal complaint was preferred against certain Brethren for forming and assembling under the denomination of ancient Masons, and pronouncing themselves independent of this society, and not subject to the laws or to the authority of the Grand Master. Dr. Manningham, the D.G.M., observed that "such meetings were not only contrary to the laws of Masonry, but an insult to the Grand Master and to the whole of the Free and Accepted Masons; as they tended to introduce the novelties and conceits of opinionative persons, and to create a belief that there have been other societies of Masons more ancient than this society." After much deliberation, it was unanimously resolved, "That the meeting of Brethren under any deno-

---

Heseltine, Esq.; John Allen, Esq.; Bartholomew Ruspini, Esq.; Francis Coust, Esq. ; Sir Herbert Mackworth, Bart.

mination of Masons, without a legal power and
authority from the Grand Lodge of England for
the time being, is inconsistent with the honour
and interest of Masonry, and an open violation
of the established laws of the Order." [s]

This resolution was followed up by the erasure
of twenty-one Lodges from the list, for irregu-
larity; and particular mention is made of one of
these Lodges, which was most active in its propo-
gation of the schism, held at the Ben Jonson's
Head, in Spitalfields, and its fourteen members
were all expelled the society by name. Such
prompt and decisive proceedings were met by
a public remonstrance on the part of the ancients,
couched in the following language:—"A Lodge
at the Ben Jonson's Head, in Pelham-street,
Spitalfields, was composed mostly of ancient Masons, though under the modern constitution.
Some of them had been abroad, and received
extraordinary benefits on account of ancient
Masonry; therefore they agreed to practise ancient
Masonry on every third lodge night." This
avowal contains an indirect allusion to the Continental innovations from which the Royal Arch
had been concocted; for all the new systems
claimed to be derived from some ancient system
of Scotch Masonry, which, in fact, never existed.
" Upon one of these nights, some modern Masons
attempted to visit them, but were refused admit-
tance. The persons so refused laid a formal com-

[s] Minutes of the Grand Lodge, March 20, 1755

D

plaint before the modern Grand Lodge, then held at the Devil Tavern, near Temple Bar. The said Grand Lodge, though *incapable of judging the propriety* or impropriety of such refusal (because, I suppose, they knew nothing of the Royal Arch), not being ancient Masons, ordered that the Ben Jonson's Lodge should admit all sorts of Masons without distinction, and upon non-compliance with that order, they were censured.

" The persons thus censured, drew up, printed, and published, a manifesto, and Mason's creed, which did honour to their heads and hearts. The following lines are copied from the preface to their pamphlet :—' Whereas, the genuine spirit of Masonry seems to be greatly on the decline, that the Craft is in imminent danger from false Brethren; and whereas, its very fundamentals have of late been attacked, and a revolution from its ancient principles, &c., it has been thought necessary by certain persons who have the welfare of the Craft at heart, to publish the following little pamphlet, by means of which it is hoped the ignorant may be instructed, the lukewarm inspirited, and the irregular reformed.' Every real, that is, every ancient Mason, who read those publications, was convinced of the injustice done to the Ben Jonson's Lodge in censuring them for having done their duty; a duty which they owed to God, and to themselves; *and a business with which their judges, the then modern Grand Lodge, were totally unacquainted.* Nevertheless, censure was passed, and a minute thereof preserved in the archives, from whence it was published as one of the legislative orders on their records." [9]

[9] "Ahiman Rezon," p. 12.

CHAPTER VII.

EXPULSION OF THE ATHOL MASONS.

MATTERS went on in this state for some years, both parties increasing in numbers and respectability; until the ancients procured the high patronage of the Duke of Athol, the Grand Master elect of Scotland, who undertook the office of Grand Master, in 1776; and the opposition, which was now carried on upon more equal terms, had the effect of stimulating the zeal of the Fraternity on both sides; and the number of Lodges was gradually augmented by the issue of new warrants from each of the rival Grand Lodges. In 1777, Lord Petre, the Grand Master of the modern section, again brought the subject before the Grand Lodge; and on the 17th of April, the following resolutions were unanimously agreed to:—"That no Lodge can assemble without a warrant from the Grand Master, and that the persons who have assembled, and still continue to assemble as Masons, by virtue of a power from a pretended Grand Lodge, established in London a few years since, and which is now said to exist under the patronage of the Duke of Athol, are not to be countenanced or acknowledged by any regular Mason under the constitution of England, on pain of forfeiting the privileges of the society; the said convention being a gross insult to the Grand Master and to every Lodge under his auspices; and the more effectually to discourage these illegal conventions, that no regular Mason shall be present at them, or give any sanction to their proceedings. That it is the opinion of this Grand Lodge, that the persons calling themselves ancient Masons, and now assembling in England, or elsewhere, under the sanction of the Duke of Athol, are not to be considered as Masons, nor are their meetings to be countenanced or acknowledged by any Lodge or Mason acting under our authority. That this censure shall not extend to any Mason who shall produce a certificate, or give other satisfactory proof of his having been made a Mason in a regular Lodge under the constitution of Scotland, Ireland, or any foreign Grand Lodge, in alliance with the Grand Lodge of England."

These resolutions produced the famous letter of Laurence Dermott, the D.G.M. of the ancients, in which he propounds the following queries:—
Q. Whether Freemasonry, as practised in ancient Lodges, is universal? *A.* Yes. *Q.* Whether what is called modern Masonry is universal? *A.* No. *Q.* Whether there is any material difference between the ancient and modern? *A.* A great deal; because an ancient Mason can not only make himself known to his Brother, but, in case of necessity, can discover his very thoughts to

him in the presence of a modern, without being
able to distinguish that either of them are Freemasons.[1]   *Q.* Whether a modern Mason may,
with safety, communicate all his secrets to an
ancient Mason?   *A.* Yes.   *Q.* Whether an
ancient Mason may, with the like safety, communicate all his secrets to a modern Mason, without farther ceremony?   *A.* No; for, as a science
comprehends an art, though an art cannot comprehend a science, even so ancient Masonry contains everything valuable amongst the moderns,
as well as many other things that cannot be
revealed without additional ceremonies (the Royal
Arch for instance).   *Q.* Whether a person made
in a modern manner, and not after the ancient
custom of the Craft, has a right to be called Free
and Accepted, according to the intent and meaning of the words?   *A.* His being unqualified to
appear in a Master's Lodge, according to the
universal system of Masonry, renders the appellation improper.   *Q.* Whether it is possible to

---

[1] An annotator makes the following observation on the
above :—"The author of 'Ahiman Rezon' has stated that he
could convey his mind to an ancient Mason in the presence of a
modern Mason, without the latter knowing whether either of
them were Masons. He further asserted that he was able,
with a few Masonic implements — *i. e.*, two squares and a
common gavel, or hammer—to convey any word or sentence of
his own, or the immediate dictations of a stranger, to a skilful
and intelligent Freemason of the ancient order, without
speaking, writing, or noise ; and that to any distance when the
parties can see each other, and at the same time be able to
distinguish squares from circles." This Masonic system of
cypher-writing is now well understood.

initiate or introduce a modern Mason into the Royal Arch Lodge (the very essence of Masonry), without making him go through the ancient ceremonies? *A.* No. *Q.* Whether the present members of modern Lodges are blameable for deviating so. much from the old Landmarks? *A.* No; because the innovation was made in the reign of George I., and the new form was delivered as orthodox to the present members. *Q.* Therefore, as it is natural for each party to maintain the orthodoxy of their Masonic preceptors, how shall we distinguish the original and most useful system? *A. The number of ancient Masons abroad, compared with the moderns,* prove the universality of the old Order, and the utility thereof appears by the love and respect shown to the Brethren, in consequence of their superior abilities in conversing with, and distinguishing the Masons of all countries and denominations, a circumstance peculiar to ancient Masons." [2]

It will be unnecessary to enquire whether all this is consistent with the requirements of Masonic duty. It is clear that disobedience is a breach of Masonic law. The very essence of the institution

---

[2] "Ahiman Rezon," p. 18. The reference to the number of foreign Masons in the last answer contains an evident allusion to the several systems of Scotch Masonry, which were at that time prevalent in France and Germany; all of which were confidently proclaimed to be ancient, when, in fact, the inventors were still living. The number of Brethren who were contented to practise unalloyed symbolical Masonry—the only system which possessed any real claims to antiquity—on the Continent were comparatively few.

is founded on obedience to authority; and this
once forfeited, led to division, anarchy, and dispute. But good frequently springs out of evil.
The bee has a sting, but it produces honey.
These movements excited the attention of the
Fraternity, and also of the public. Ancient feelings, which had long been dormant in some of
the initiated, began to revive, and they renewed
their connection with the Lodges they had abandoned. Lukewarm Brethren became partizans
on either side, and Freemasonry reaped the
benefit of these misunderstandings by an increase
both in numbers and influence. A more active
study of its principles led to a greater perfection
in the science, and many initiations took place
amongst persons who had not previously given
the institution a serious thought. Thus the ranks
of both ancient and modern were increased, and
the funds of benevolence for the widow and orphan
augmented from new and unexpected sources :
a result which cemented the popularity of the
Order. Its beauties and excellencies were placed
in a clearer and more prominent point of view,
and the public became convinced that, though
the two hostile parties might differ on some
unimportant points of discipline, both were pur-
suing the same laudable course,—the investigation
of science, and the benefit of mankind.

About this time, a treaty of alliance and con-
federation was effected by the ancients with the
Grand Lodges of Scotland and Ireland, under an
impression that the ancient rites of Masonry were

exclusively practised by them, and that the English Grand Lodge had departed from the primitive Landmarks, and deteriorated the system by modern innovations.[3] In this treaty, it was mutually agreed, that each Grand Lodge should transmit to the others, an account of their proceedings; and that all such information or correspondence should be conveyed in the most respectful terms, such as might suit the honour and dignity of the respective Grand Lodges.

---

[3] A correspondent to one of the London papers, in June, 1783, states, rather strongly, that the ancients "having prevailed on some of the Brethren from Scotland and Ireland to attend their meetings, and inducing them to believe that the ancient rites of Masonry were only practised by them, and that the regular Lodges had deviated from the ancient landmarks, they obtained through this channel a friendly intercourse with the Grand Lodges of both kingdoms, and a treaty of alliance was inadvertently formed between these Grand Lodges and this irregular society. Neither of these respectable bodies, had the real origin of those seceders from the regular fraternity been known, would have permitted their authority to sanction an infringement of the Constitutions of Masonry, to which all Masons are bound, or an encroachment on the established legislature of the fraternity in this kingdom." As this assertion was not contradicted, there appears to have been some truth in it.

CHAPTER VIII.

UNION OF THE TWO SECTIONS.

THE two societies continued to practise Masonry according to their respective views, until the year 1801, when it appears that several members of the modern Craft were in the habit of attending the meetings of the ancient Lodges, and rendering their assistance in the ceremonies of making, passing, and raising; by which conduct they became amenable to the laws of Masonry. Complaints to this effect were formally preferred, and the Grand Lodge found itself obliged to notice the proceedings, and after some deliberation, the erring Brethren were attainted, and allowed three months to prepare their defence. It does not appear that the Grand Lodge had any intention of making an example of the offenders; on the contrary, in accordance with the amiable spirit of Masonry, it displayed an anxiety to heal the divisions by which the Order had been so long distracted; and used its utmost efforts to effect an union of the two bodies; thus closing for ever the dissensions that proved a bar to the divine exercise of Brotherly love. For this purpose, a committee was appointed, with Lord Moira, the

D.G.M., at its head, who declared, on accepting his appointment as a member of the committee, that "he should consider the day on which a coalition should be formed, as one of the most fortunate in his life; and that he was empowered by the Prince of Wales, G.M., to say that His Royal Highness's arms would ever be open to all the Masons in the kingdom indiscriminately." As a mutual concession, the D.G.M. of the ancients publicly promised, on his own part, and in the names of his two friends, against whom charges had been exhibited, that if the Grand Lodge would extend their indulgence to them, they would use their utmost exertions to effect an union between the two societies; and he pledged himself to the Grand Lodge that it should be accomplished.

It does not appear, however, that he adopted any measures which might tend to heal the breach; for, on the 9th of February, 1803, it was represented to the Grand Lodge, that the irregular Masons still continued refractory; and that, so far from soliciting readmission into the Craft, they had not taken any steps to effect an union; their conduct was, therefore, deemed highly censurable, and the laws of the Grand Lodge were ordered to be enforced against them. It was unanimously resolved, that the persons who were opposed to the union of the two Grand Lodges be expelled the society; and also for countenancing and supporting a set of persons calling themselves ancient Masons and holding Lodges in this kingdom without the authority of his Royal Highness the Prince of Wales, the Grand Master, duly elected by this Grand Lodge. That whenever it shall appear that any Masons under the English constitution shall in future attend or countenance any Lodge or meeting of persons calling themselves ancient Masons, under the sanction of any person claiming the title of Grand Master of England, who shall not have been duly elected in this Grand Lodge, the laws of the society shall not only be strictly enforced against them, but their names shall be erased from the list, and transmitted to all the regular Lodges under the constitution of England.

These differences became at length so irksome, that the most influential Brethren in both divisions of the Craft, were earnestly desirous of an union.[1]

[1] This was strongly urged in a letter to the Duke of Athol, published by Bro. Daniell in 1801. "From a close and attentive observation," says he, "aided by frequent conversations with several of the most worthy and respectable members of that society, I am warranted to assert that an union has long been desired by them with an ardour equal to my own. Under all these circumstances, can it be supposed, my Lord, that you, as a regular Mason, when you are informed of the origin of the institution which I am fully persuaded you patronize from the purest motives ; can it, I say, be supposed that you or any nobleman would lend his name to support or countenance any society, however praiseworthy their motives might have appeared, who meet in direct violation of the laws and government of the Fraternity ? No, my Lord, your public character is too well known, your zeal for the welfare of the country is too manifest, and your attachment to the royal family too deeply rooted, to admit of deviation. Therefore, I trust your feelings will coincide with my own, and that you will really conceive

The first actual step which was taken to produce that effect originated with the Earl of Moira, in the negotiation of a treaty of alliance between the English Grand Lodge, of which he was the D.G.M., and the Grand Lodge of Scotland, under the Grand Mastership of the Earls of Aboyne and Dalhousie. At the grand festival of St. Andrew, holden at Edinburgh, November 13, 1803, the Earl of Dalhousie on the throne, Lord Moira introduced the question of the English schism, and explained the conduct of the Grand Lodge of England towards the ancient Masons. He stated that "the hearts and arms of the Grand Lodge had ever been open for the reception of their seceding Brethren, who had obstinately refused to acknowledge their faults, and return to the bosom of their mother Lodge; and that, though the Grand Lodge of England differed in a few trifling observances from that of Scotland, they had ever entertained for Scottish Masons that affection and regard which it is the object of Freemasonry to cherish, and the duty of Freemasons to feel." His lordship's speech was received by the Brethren with loud and reiterated applause; a most unequivocal mark of their approbation of its sentiments.[2]

what honour, what peculiar satisfaction, and what heartfelt pleasure it would give you, to bring that society which you have lately patronized under the royal banner." — *Masonic Union*, pp. 23, 27.

[2] Laurie thus expresses himself on the subject:—"In the general history of Freemasonry, we have already given an account of the schism which took place in the Grand Lodge of

An official despatch on the above subject from the same nobleman, was read at the Quarterly Communication, in April, 1805; and it was resolved, " That as the Grand Lodge of Scotland has expressed, through the Earl of Moira, its earnest wish to be on terms of confidential communication with the Grand Lodge of England, under the authority of the Prince of Wales, this Grand Lodge, therefore, ever desirous to concur in a fraternal intercourse with the regular Masons, doth meet that disposition with the utmost cordiality of sentiment, and requests the honour of the acting Grand Master to make such declarations, in their name, to the Grand Lodge of Scotland."

England by the secession of a number of men who, calling themselves ancient Masons, invidiously bestowed upon the Grand Lodge the appellation of moderns. These ancient Masons, who certainly merit blame as the active promoters of the schism, chose for their Grand Master, in the year 1772, his Grace the Duke of Athol, who was then Grand Master elect for Scotland. From this circumstance, more than from any particular predilection on the part of the Grand Lodge of Scotland for the ancient Masons, the most friendly intercourse has always subsisted between the two Grand Lodges ; and the Scottish Masons, from their union with the ancients, imbibed the same prejudices against the Grand Lodge of England, arising merely from some trifling innovations in ceremonial observances which had been inconsiderately authorized. From these causes, the Grand Lodges of Scotland and England, though the Brethren of both were admitted into each other's Lodges, never cherished that mutual and friendly intercourse which, by the principles of Freemasonry, they were bound to institute and preserve. Such was the relative condition of the Grand Lodge of Scotland, and that of England under the Prince of Wales, on the day of the present election."—*Hist. of Freemasonry,* p. 294.

The circumstances which led to this good understanding were detailed by Lord Moira, from his place on the throne of the Grand Lodge, at the Quarterly Communication, in February, 1806. His lordship stated that, during his residence in Edinburgh, he had visited the Grand Lodge of Scotland, and taken an opportunity of explaining to it the extent and importance of this Grand Lodge, and also the origin and situation of those Masons in England who met under the authority of the Duke of Athol; that the Brethren of the Grand Lodge of Scotland he found to have been greatly misinformed upon the point; having always been led to think that this society was of recent date, and of no magnitude; but now, being thoroughly convinced of their error, they were desirous that the strictest union and most intimate communication should subsist between this Grand Lodge and the Grand Lodge of Scotland; and, as the first step towards so important an object, and in testimony of the wishes of the Scottish Masons, his Royal Highness the Prince of Wales had been unanimously elected Grand Master of Scotland. That the said Grand Lodge had expressed its concern that any difference should subsist among the Masons of England, and that the Lodges meeting under the sanction of the Duke of Athol should have withdrawn themselves from the protection of the ancient Grand Lodge of England; but hoped that measures might be adopted to produce a reconciliation; and that the Lodges now holding irregular meetings, would return to their duty, and again be received into the bosom of the Fraternity. That, in reply, his lordship had stated his firm belief, that this Grand Lodge would readily concur in any measures that might be proposed for establishing union and harmony among the general body of Masons; yet, that after the rejection of the propositions made by this Grand Lodge, three years ago, it could not now, consistent with its honour, or the dignity of its illustrious Grand Master, make any further advances; but that, as it still retained its disposition to promote the general interests of the Craft, it would always be open to accept of the mediation of the Grand Lodge of Scotland, if it should think proper to interfere.

On this representation, it was resolved that a letter should be written to the Grand Lodge of Scotland, expressive of the desire of this Grand Lodge, that the strictest union may subsist between the Grand Lodge of England and the Grand Lodge of Scotland; and that the actual Masters and Wardens of the Lodges under the authority of the Grand Lodge of Scotland, who may be in London, on producing proper testimonials, shall have a seat in this Grand Lodge, and be permitted to vote on all occasions. A communication was subsequently received from the Grand Lodge of Ireland, desiring to co-operate with this Grand Lodge in every particular which might support the authority necessary to be maintained by the representative body of the whole Craft over an individual Lodge; and pledging itself not to countenance, or receive as a Brother, any person standing under the interdict of the Grand Lodge of England for Masonic transgression. It was therefore resolved, in Quarterly Communication, "That the acting Grand Master be requested to express to the Grand Lodge of Ireland, the sense which this Grand Lodge entertains of so cordial a communication." [3]

These public declarations of the Grand Lodges of Scotland and Ireland, appear to have made a strong impression on the ancient Masons; [4] who, entertaining an apprehension that their authority would be altogether superseded by such a coalition, now became anxious to complete the desired reunion of the two bodies; and their overtures were received in a Masonic spirit by the authorities of the constitutional section of the Craft. In the

[3] Preston's Illustr., pp. 337, 340.

[4] This impression was strengthened by a communication from the Grand Lodge of Sweden, in which the hereditary Prince and G.M. thus expresses himself : — "To contract an intimate, sincere, and permanent tie between the national Grand Lodge of Sweden and that of England has long been ardently our object. . . . . The uniformity of situation, as well as the fundamental principles of the Craft, which we equally profess, authorize us to consolidate and draw closer a confidence, friendship, and reciprocal union between two bodies, whose common object is the good of humanity, who mutually consider friendship as the nerve, and the love of our neighbour as the pivot of all our labours. . . . . This union being once established between two nations who reciprocally esteem each other, and who are both known to possess the requisite qualities of all Free and Accepted Masons, it will consolidate for ever the foundation of the Masonic Temple, whose majestic edifice will endure to future ages."

year 1809, it was resolved, "That it is not necessary to continue in force any longer those measures which were resorted to in or about the year 1739, respecting irregular Masons; and we, therefore, enjoin the Lodges *to revert to the ancient landmarks of the society.*" An occasional Lodge was then appointed, called the Lodge of Promulgation, as a preparatory step to carrying out the union of ancient and modern Masons.

This concession was responded to on the part of the ancients by the resignation of the Duke of Athol, as G.M., and the appointment of his Royal Highness the Duke of Kent to that office; who publicly declared at his installation, in 1813, that he had consented to accept the office solely with a view of promoting and effecting an union between the ancient and modern sections of the Craft. His Royal Highness the Duke of Sussex being, at that period, the G.M. of the constitutional Masons, the two royal Brothers, with the advice and assistance of three learned Masons from amongst the members of each division, framed a series of articles for the future government of the United Grand Lodge.[5] On the one side were, Waller Rodwell Wright, Arthur Tegart, and James Deans, Esqrs.; and on the other,

---

[5] And it was mutually agreed that the property of the two Fraternities, whether freehold, leasehold, or personal, shall remain sacredly appropriate to the purposes for which it was created; and that it shall constitute one great fund, by which the blessed object of Masonic benevolence may be more extensively obtained.

Thomas Harper, James Perry, and James Agar, Esqrs. The articles were signed, ratified, and confirmed, and the seal of the respective Grand Lodges affixed on the 1st of December, 1813.[6] It was here agreed, "for the purpose of establishing and securing this perfect uniformity in all the warranted Lodges, and to place all the members of both Fraternities on the level of equality on the day of re-union," that nine expert Master Masons from each of the Fraternities, should hold a Lodge of Reconciliation, for the purpose of settling the ceremonies, lectures, and discipline, on such a basis that " there shall be the most perfect unity of obligation, &c., so that but one pure unsullied system, according to the genuine landmarks, laws, and conditions of the Craft, shall be maintained, upheld, and practised, throughout the Masonic world."[7] When all these preliminaries were settled, the event was commemorated by a general Grand Festival;[8] and

[6] At this Grand Lodge a letter was read from Bro. Laurie, Grand Secretary of Scotland, transmitting Resolutions of that Grand Lodge, in answer to a letter already sent by the M.W. the Grand Masters of the two Grand Lodges, announcing to them the happy event of the union, and requesting them to appoint a deputation, agreeably to Art. IV. of the Act of Union. A similar letter was also read from Bro. Graham, the G. Sec. of the Grand Lodge of Ireland.

[7] Articles of Union, iii. v.

[8] At which was recited a beautiful ode, written for the occasion by Bro. Waller Rodwell Wright, in the second epode of which the following passage occurs :—

"Alas ! that e'er a cloud should rise,
    To dim the glories of thy name ;

it is confidently hoped that " the removal of all
the slight differences which have so long kept the
Brotherhood asunder, will be the means of establishing in the metropolis of the British empire,
one splendid edifice of ancient Freemasonry, to
which the whole Masonic world may confidently
look for the maintenance and preservation of the
pure principles of the Craft, as handed down to
them from time immemorial, under the protection
of the illustrious branches of the royal house of
Brunswick; and that it may produce the extension
and practice of the virtues of loyalty, morality,
brotherly love, and benevolence, which it has ever
been the great object of Freemasonry to inculcate,
and of its laws to enforce." [9]

> Or little jealousies divide
> The souls by kindred vows allied.
> But see ! while thus our rites we blend,
> The mingled sacrifice ascend,
> And borne to heaven in one united flame,
> Chase every ling'ring shadow from the skies."

---

[9] Minutes of Grand Lodge, 27th Dec., 1813.

CHAPTER IX.

PRACTICAL VARIETIES IN THE RITUALS.

AT the union of the two Grand Chapters of Royal Arch Masons in England, in 1817, the title of " United Grand Chapter " was used until 1822, when the title of "Supreme Grand Chapter" was resumed. The English Royal Arch, at present, according to the constitutions, appears to be practised as a fourth degree; for the Past Master, though now elevated into a distinct grade, attended with certain exclusive privileges, is not essential for exaltation.[1] The articles of union, however, set out with a declaration that " ancient Masonry consists of three degrees only, *including the Royal Arch;* " and the Supreme Grand Chapter still hold the doctrine that, in all things, wherein by analogy, the constitutions of Craft Masonry can be followed, they shall determine the laws of the Royal Arch. Thus the connection between Craft and Royal Arch Masonry is still maintained, although they differ in design, in

[1] Our R. A. Constitutions provide that no Mason shall be exalted to this sublime degree, unless he have been a Master Mason for twelve calendar months at the least, of which satisfactory proof shall be given.

clothing, in constitutions, and in colour; and
the proceedings are regulated by different govern-
ing bodies. In 1813, the union of Royal Arch
Masonry with the Craft Grand Lodge, being considered extremely desirable, his Royal Highness
the Duke of Sussex was invested with unlimited
powers to effect the object. On this resolution
the editor of the *Freemasons' Quarterly Review*
thus remarks:—" Well had it been for English
Freemasonry if this object had been carried out
to its fullest extent; which, at some future time,
may even yet be effected."[2] In another place
the editor remarks:—"The Royal Arch in
England is not essentially a degree, but the perfection of the third. The entire system requires
careful re-examination."[3]

There still exist in the English system some few
anomalies after all the pains which have been
bestowed upon it to make it perfect. I refer, in
the first place, to the names of the scribes. The
foundation of the second temple was laid in the
year B.C. 535; after which the building was
hindered till B.C. 520; when it went on by order
of Darius, and was dedicated B.C. 515. But Ezra
did not come up from Babylon till the reign of
Artaxerxes, B.C. 457; being fifty-eight years after
the dedication of the second temple, and seventy-
eight after the foundations were laid; and
Nehemiah was not made governor till twelve

[2] Freemasons' Quarterly Review, 1842, p. 411.
[3] Ibid. 1843, p. 464.

years later than that. They could not then have been participators with Z, at the rebuilding of that sacred edifice. It appears probable that this anachronism may have arizen from Ezra having recorded in his first six chapters what happened from sixty to eighty years before his time; and from the name of Nehemiah, evidently, as Dean Prideaux shows, a different person of the same name, appearing in Ezra ii. 2, as one of those who accompanied Z out of Babylon. Another particular, about the propriety of which I entertain some doubts, is in the arrangement of the three Principals, Z, H, J. I think the order would be more correctly Z, J, H; not only because J is recorded, in the scripture account, as taking an active part with Z, but also because the office of Priest was acknowledged to be superior to that of Prophet. And there is another consideration which, in this case, is of some importance, that our Lord entered *first* upon the prophetical office; *second*, on the sacerdotal, viz., at Golgotha; and *third*, on the regal, viz., from Olivet.* These and some other anomalies, which need not be specified, I should imagine, might easily be amended.

Our Irish Brethren entertain an opinion that the English mode mixes up two distinct matters; and that the *time* used in England for the

* Thus we read in the Symbolical Lecture, that the bearings on the banners denote the regal, the prophetical, and the sacerdotal offices, all of which were and still ought to be conferred, and in a peculiar manner accompanied with the possession of particular secrets.

events of the Arch, belongs properly to another
degree; *i.e.* the Knight of the Sword and the
East; while some intelligent Brethren consider
the Royal Arch degree to be really and truly a
part of the Order of the East. Their system
consists of three degrees: the Excellent, Super-
Excellent, and Royal Arch; as a preliminary step
to which the Past Master's degree is indispensable.
The two first are given in Lodges, by a Master
and Wardens; and the last in a Chapter governed
by three Principals. The Excellent and Super-
Excellent appear to refer exclusively to the legation of Moses, as we shall see hereafter. After
the candidate has received these, the Chapter is
opened, the events of the Arch are transacted, and
the Sublime Secrets disclosed to them.

In Scotland, great changes and innovations
appear to have occurred in Freemasonry at a very
early period; for in the charter granted by the
Masons to William St. Clair, of Roslin, about A.D.
1600, mention is made of "many false corruptions
and imperfections in the Craft," having been
introduced for want of "ane patron and protec-
tor;" and in the confirmation of this charter, in
1630, the Brethren repeat that "there are very
many corruptions and imperfectious risen and
ingenerit, both amongst ourselves and in our said
vocations." And again, in the same document,
they give as a reason for the renewal of the
charter, that it had become necessary "for repa-
ration of the ruines and manifold corruptions and
enormities in our said Craft, done by unskilful

persons thereintill." What these corruptions were, is not specified; but it is quite clear, from the apprehensions of the Fraternity, that fears were entertained lest the old principles of the Order should be entirely extinguished. It is doubtful whether the Grand Scotch degree of St. Andrew was known in Scotland at the time when our Royal Arch was established, as it is a foreign degree, and, at present, forms the twenty-eighth of the Rite Ancien et Accepté. Its ceremonies approximate nearer than any other to the English Royal Arch, although they differ widely from it. In 1755, mention is made of the Glasgow Royal Arch, and four years later, the Stirling Royal Arch; and subsequently, we find the Ayr Royal Arch, the Maybole Royal Arch, &c.; but how they were constituted, or what rites were practised in them, is, at present, very uncertain. In the best rituals used in Scotland, the degree of Excellent Master, comprehending three steps —improperly called veils, for the temple had but one veil [5]—is supposed to be given at Babylon, as a test, to prevent mere Master Masons from participating in the privilege of building the second temple; which was confined to those who were liberated by Cyrus, and consequently *returned from Babylon.* It was, therefore, a temporary degree; but during the building an incident occurred on which the Royal Arch was founded;

[5] In our own system the pedestal is veiled during the ceremony of exaltation, and also the cubical block of marble in the vault.

and hence the Scotch Masons keep up the Excellent as a sort of introduction to it.

In America, we find an essential variation from any other system of the Royal Arch. The names of the officers vary materially, as also do the ceremonies. As in Ireland, it constitutes the seventh degree, although the intermediate steps are different. In Ireland they are, 1. E.A.P. 2. F.C. 3. M.M. 4. P.M. 5. Excellent. 6. Super-Excellent. 7. Royal Arch; while in America the fourth is Mark Master.[6] 5. P.M.[7] 6. Most Excellent Master. 7. Royal Arch. Until the year 1797, no Grand Chapter of Royal Arch Masons was organized in America. Before this period, and from the year 1764, when it was first introduced, probably by Stephen Morin, who had been in England, and there received the degree, a competent number of Companions, possessed of sufficient abilities, under the sanction of a Master's warrant, proceeded to exercise the rights and

[6] In the National Convention, or Meeting of Delegates from the Grand Lodge of the United States, at Baltimore, in 1843, it was decreed that in processions Mark Masters should rank next to Senior Wardens. The several degrees of Mark Master, Present or Past Master, and Most Excellent Master, are given in the Chapter; and a Master Mason who applies for these degrees must of necessity enter the Chapter; and sometimes the four degrees are given at one time. When this is the case, he is balloted for only once, viz., in the *Mark Master's Degree.*

[7] Dalcho says that in America they communicate the secret of the chair to such applicants as have not already received it previous to their admission into the Sublime Lodges; but they are informed that it does not give them rank as Past Masters in the Grand Lodge.

privileges of Royal Arch Chapters whenever they thought it expedient and proper; although in most cases the approbation of a neighbouring Chapter was usually obtained.[8] "This unrestrained mode of proceeding," says Webb,[9] "was subject to many inconveniences; unsuitable characters might be admitted; *irregularities in the mode of working introduced;*[10] the purposes of the society perverted; and thus the Order was degraded by falling into the hands of those who might be regardless of the reputation of the institution." And this may be one reason why the ceremonies differ so essentially from those which are used in this country.

The officers of a Chapter in America are, a High-Priest, King, Scribe, Captain of the Host, Principal Sojourner, Royal Arch Captain, Grand Masters of the 1st, 2nd, and 3rd veils, Secretary, and Treasurer.[11] The warrants issued to private

[8] As Morin was a Grand Inspector-General of the Continental degrees, he would have conferred the Royal Arch in his consistory if he had not found it practised under the sanction of blue Masonry in England; which is a presumptive proof that a regular Grand Chapter of the Royal Arch had not been formed by the Ancients in 1764.

[9] Monitor, p. 178.

[10] And also irregularities in the manufacture of spurious degrees. Thus, for instance, we find on the Continent twenty degrees of Apprentice, twenty-three of Fellow Craft or Compagnon, and sixty-five of Master Mason.

[11] The R. A. Chapters of this country consist of three Principals, who, when in Chapter assembled, are to be considered conjointly as the Master, and each severally as a Master, two Scribes, three Sojourners, Treasurer, Registrar, Sword-Bearer, Standard-Bearer, Director of Ceremonies, and Organist.

Chapters contain an authority to open and hold
Lodges of Most Excellent, Past, and Mark Master
Masons; the High Priest, King, and Scribe, for
the time being, to act as the Master and Wardens
of the said Lodges.[12]

Thus have I detailed the chief varieties in the
different systems of Royal Arch Masonry. My
reason for being thus particular is, to show that
the differences are organic, and consequently the
degree cannot be of any great antiquity; for if it
were, there would exist more uniformity in practice, as is the case with. the symbolical degrees,
which may undoubtedly claim a very ancient
origin. I am afraid, however, that those Brethren
and Companions who have been in the habit of
valuing the Royal Arch on account of its antiquity,
will be sadly disappointed to find it thus shorn of
one of its brightest attributes.[13] But there is

---

[12] In constituting a new Chapter, the Grand High Priest uses
the following expressive form :—" By virtue of the high powers
in us vested, I do form you, my worthy companions, into a
regular Chapter of Royal Arch Masons. From henceforth you
are authorized and empowered to open and hold a Lodge of
Mark Masters, Past Masters, and Most Excellent Masters, and
a Chapter of Royal Arch Masons; and to do and perform all
such things as thereunto may appertain ; conforming in all
your doings to the constitution of the General Grand Royal
Arch Chapter : and may the God of your fathers be with you,
and guide and direct you in all your doings."

[13] I find myself in the same predicament as Sir William
Drummond describes in his preface to the " Origines," when he
says—" In questions unconnected with sacred and important
interests, men are rarely very anxious to discriminate exactly
between truth and fiction ; *and few of us would, probably, be
much pleased with the result,* could it now be certainly proved

rather cause for congratulation than regret; for what can be fairer or more desirable than truth? The degree loses none of its excellencies by being shown to be of modern origin. If its claims to antiquity were not well founded, its advocates were maintaining a fallacy; and often found themselves in a dilemma, when proofs were demanded which it was impossible to produce. The above arguments will remove many doubts, by at least placing the matter in a clearer point of view, even if they be not allowed the merit of absolute demonstration. And as the case has been candidly stated, without any offensive reflections on the parties concerned in the transaction, who, it is believed, were conscientiously persuaded that the design would confer dignity on the Order, no exceptions can be taken, on the score of partiality, to the end I have had in view, which is the discovery of truth.

I have been anxious to clear up this dark problem in the history of Masonry; and if I have been successful, the time I have employed in the investigation has not been ill bestowed. At any

that Troy never existed, and that Thebes, with its hundred gates, was no more than a populous village. It is, perhaps, still with a secret wish to be convinced against our judgment that we reject as fables the stories told us of the Grecian Hercules, or of the Persian Rustem, and that we assign to the heroes and the giants of early times the strength and stature of ordinary men." So it is with our Royal Arch. We wish to be convinced, even against our judgment, that it is an ancient degree, because our prejudices have long cherished so pleasing an idea.

rate, the hints I have thrown out may be of some use to others in discovering the origin of this sublime degree; and even in that case the labour and research have not been altogether misapplied. If I have led the inquiries into a proper track, I shall have accomplished that which will shield me from censure.

> Interdum speciosa locis, morataque recte
> Fabula, nullius veneris, sine pondere et arte,
> Valdius oblectat populum, meliusque moratur,
> Quam versus inopes rerum nugæque canoræ.[14]

It must be evident to every candid reader, that in these suggestions I have been actuated by no other motives than those which have influenced a long and active life in the cause of Freemasonry; viz., a high veneration for its sublime qualities; a love of its principles, not to be subdued by any earthly influence; and an arduous desire to remove every objectionable impediment. I have devoted the humble talents which I possess to the dissemination of its beauties, under many disadvantages; and I trust that I have contributed, in some slight degree, to increase its influence, and promote its popularity in the world. In my anxiety to place it on the pinnacle of true greatness, based on Charity, crowned with Wisdom, Strength, and Beauty, and receiving the universal testimony of human applause, I have been induced to investigate its claims to public approbation; because I think it is fairly entitled to that flattering

---

[14] Hor. de Art. Poet. v. 320.

eulogium which was pronounced on the writers of the English Augustan period of literature. "Such an institution as this, in a Roman age, would have been more glorious than a public triumph; statues would have been raised, and medals would have been struck, in honour of its supporters. Antiquity had so high a sense of gratitude for the communication of knowledge, that they worshipped their law-givers, and deified the fathers of science. How then must they have acknowledged services like these, where every man grew wiser and better by the fine instruction." [15]

[15] From an Essay sacred to the memory of Sir Richard Steele.

THE ORIGIN OF THE
ENGLISH ROYAL ARCH DEGREE.

———•◦•———

PART II.

THE PROGRESSIVE RITUALS, DOCTRINES, AND SYMBOLS OF THE ROYAL ARCH.

CHAPTER I.

THE FIRST ROYAL ARCH RITUAL.

THE Royal Arch was styled by its fabricators the Fourth Degree, although at its primitive adoption it was considered by them, as it is at present in this country, a completion of the third, and essentially Christian;[1] for the system, as originated by the Brethren who seceded from the constitutional Grand Lodge in 1739, was avowedly Johannite, as is evidenced by their peculiar ceremonies and lectures, of which I subjoin a brief analysis. And I shall further show that the first germ of the degree, as it was designed by them, and practised at the "Ben Jonson's Head," was an unauthorized remodification of the Third Degree, to suit their own purpose of placing an insurmountable barrier between themselves and their constitutional Brethren, and hence differing, according to their own account, "exceedingly

[1] "Masons are very often designated," says Bro. Sir Osborne Gibbs, P.G.S.W. for Dorset, at the P.G. Meeting in 1848, "as a body of Infidels, Deists, Unitarians, and the like. But this is both false and unfounded. I would most emphatically assert that it is a Christian institution—Christian in every sense of the word; and I am most anxious to convince you that it is so."

in makings, ceremonies, knowledge, masonic language, and installations; so much so, that they always had been, and still continued to be, two distinct societies, totally independent of each other." [2] And they began by denominating the Third Degree " The Geometrick Master," [3] and ended by styling it " The Royal Arch."

As their method of conferring this degree has been obsolete for more than a century, and contained only a distant resemblance to the legitimate ceremonies now in use, there can be no impropriety in giving, as a curiosity, a brief sketch of the unsatisfactory jumble which was imposed on the Brethren as " Ancient Masonry," although it was undoubtedly a modern innovation. And therefore they were perfectly justified in asserting the ignorance of the constitutional Masons

---

[2] Ahiman Rezon, xxx. Ed. 1818.

[3] The following address was made to the Candidate after he had been passed to the Degree of a Fellowcraft. "From the portions of Holy Scripture which I have now read unto you, you must perceive that the science of Geometry is essentially necessary to constitute an expert Mason, because so magnificent and glorious an edifice could not have been erected without a complete knowledge of architecture, which is a science founded on the basis of Geometry. Without Geometry, how could the stones and timber have been so squared and prepared, in the quarry and in the forest, as to have fitted into their proper places when taken to, and put together in Jerusalem. If you would therefore advance in the arts and sciences, let me recommend to you very strongly, to give more attention to the science of Geometry than you have hitherto done. It affords many subjects of meditation on the wisdom, power, and goodness of the Grand Architect of the universe, who out of nothing created all things by his Almighty Word."

respecting its genuine principles. It was, indeed, impossible that they could be otherwise; nor, if they had known it, would they have thought it expedient to introduce it into their Lodges. However, as it contains the first faint glimmerings of the Royal Arch Degree, the outline may be acceptable to the fraternity of the present day, many of whom will have no difficulty in filling it up.

The degree was called the "Rite Ancien de Bouillon," and was conferred in two separate divisions, the first part closing with the O. B. (which had no penalty), and the communication of the Pass Word; and the latter, with a description of the Masonic Telegraph, and the address of St. John the Evangelist. The R. W. Master was robed in scarlet, and crowned as a king, being the representative of King Solomon; the Senior Warden in robes of purple, and also crowned, to represent Hiram, King of Tyre; and the Junior Warden attired in flowing garments of a sable colour, as H. A. B. They are thus represented in the frontispiece of the Ahiman Rezon, and are accompanied by Moses, Aholiab, and Bezaleel, Zerubbabel, Haggai, and Jeshua, clad in a similar manner; although the latter personages were not at first introduced into the degree.

The guide or conductor acted throughout the entire ceremonies as one of three candidates, a less number not being eligible.[4] Should there be

---

[4] "At the destruction of Jerusalem by Nebuchadnezzar, three Most Excellent Masters were carried captives to Babylon,

only one candidate, some other Brother was added, along with the guide, to complete the number. The Lodge was opened in the Second or Fellowcraft's Degree, and when that ceremony was completed, the Senior Warden retired, leaving his chair vacant.

The candidates were then introduced and approved, and after some preliminary ceremonies, which I pass over, their conductor addressed the Junior Warden thus : " Worshipful Sir, we make

where they remained seventy years, and were liberated by Cyrus, King of Persia. They returned to Jerusalem to assist in rebuilding the Temple, after travelling over rugged roads on foot. They arrived at the outer veil of the Tabernacle, which was erected near the ruins of the Temple. This Tabernacle was an oblong square, enclosed by four cross-veils or curtains, and divided into separate apartments by other four cross-veils, including the west-end veil or entrance. The veils were parted in the centre, and guarded by four guards with drawn swords. At the east-end of the Tabernacle, Haggai, Jeshua, and Zerubbabel usually sat in grand council, to examine all who wished to be employed in the noble and glorious work of rebuilding the Temple. Since that time every Chapter of Royal Arch Masons, if properly formed, represents the Tabernacle erected by our ancient brethren near the ruins of King Solomon's Temple. These three Most Excellent Masters, on their arrival, were introduced to the Grand Council, and being furnished with tools, they were directed to commence their labours at the north-east corner of the ruins of the old Temple, and to clear away and remove the rubbish, in order to lay the foundation of the new one. The Grand Council also gave them strict orders to preserve any specimens of ancient architecture which they might discover, and submit them to their inspection. Among the discoveries made by the three sojourners was a secret vault, in which they found treasures of great benefit to the Craft, &c., &c., &c." Such is the reason assigned by our companions in the United States for the necessity of a trial of candidates.

bold to wait upon you at this busy hour of the day for the purpose of humbly reminding you of the promise you were pleased to make to us some time ago. Our works are now completed, and we accordingly seek admission amongst the Geometrick Masters of the Craft."

To this request the Junior Warden replied: "The very zealous and faithful services which you have so diligently rendered these several years past, have not been forgotten by me, and you would not now have had cause to remind me of my promise, but that the Dedication of the Temple has so occupied our sovereign lord the King, as to exclude all inferior matters from his attention. Several other Craftsmen have, in like manner, applied to me this day, and I must give you the same answer as I have done to them. And I now recommend you to seek our Sovereign Grand Master in person, and I have no doubt but he will satisfy your inquiries."

They then advanced to the R. W. Master's chair, and said: "Sire, the Temple being now finished and dedicated to the true and everliving GOD, whose name be exalted, we are anxious to obtain that distinguished reward which has been graciously promised to us, of being admitted into the honourable degree of Geometrick Master Masons." To which the R. W. Master replied: "Brethren, the cause of the delay which you have experienced proceeds from the absence of our royal friend and ally, Hiram, King of Tyre, with whom we have entered into a solemn covenant not to confer in his absence this most sublime degree; and he has frequently expressed the greatest desire of being present when our faithful Craftsmen should receive the reward which is so justly their due.   Immediately after the dedication, an express reached him with such urgent intelligence as obliged him suddenly to return to his own country; but before he left, he reminded us of our covenant, and assured us that he would, with all possible despatch, hasten back to Jerusalem. If, however, you are willing to take upon yourselves the obligation of a Master Mason, and await the return of our royal ally, we may thus far comply with your request."   To which the conductor answered, in the name of the rest: "Sire, we very joyfully accept your most gracious offer, and confess ourselves extremely grateful."   The P.W. and O.B. are then communicated together with certain tokens [5] in due form, and the lodge was called from labour to refreshment.

[5] A Masonic tradition states that, at the transgression of our first parents, a certain sign or token was used, which has been perpetuated in the Order of Royal Arch Masonry. This sign was used by Moses when he came down from the Mount. It was again brought into requisition at the building of the second Temple ; and when Alexander the Great, with his victorious legions, approached the city of Jerusalem in order to destroy it, he was met by the High Priest in his pontifical habiliments, accompanied by the priests and Levites in solemn procession, who saluted him with this significant sign. It is an historical fact that Alexander was so much struck with the sight of this procession, that he did homage to God's vicegerent ; and it is said, on more questionable authority, that his reverence proceeded from the mutual recognition of Masonic brotherhood.

Thus closed the first or introductory portion of the ceremony of raising a Brother to the Sublime Degree of a Geometrick Master. The most prominent object which it presented to the senses of the candidate was undoubtedly the splendid character of the regalia worn by the presiding officers of the Lodge, which could not fail to attract his particular observation, as it constituted a pleasing and unexpected spectacle. But we of the present day, on a view of this feature, cannot help remarking a singular defect in the proceedings, by the entire absence of their symbolical application to morals, which ought to constitute one of the most essential elements in all rites and ceremonies of the Order. The colours indeed were gorgeous, but as they bore no allusion to ethics, they could scarcely be esteemed an apt appendage to a speculative institution, which professes to include the whole duty of man as a moral being, and is hence truly defined as a beautiful system of morality, veiled in allegory, and illustrated by symbols.

In our present improved version of the rite, how much more solemn and impressive are the references to colour in the addresses of the installation of the Principals of the Chapter, who represent three very different personages from the governors of Craft Masonry. These addresses include pregnant specimens of mental culture, and lessons of the purest Christian morality. As for instance :—

The blue colour of the robe forms a remarkable distinction, for it is one of the most beautiful

colours in nature, and was accordingly adopted
and worn by our ancient Brethren of Craft
Masonry as its peculiar characteristic, and is as
much distinguished for the durability of its
material or principle as by the beauty of its super-
structure. It is an emblem of universal benevolence and friendship, and instructs us that in the
mind of a Mason those virtues should be as ex-
pansive as the azure canopy of heaven itself.

The colours of this degree are purple, crimson,
and pale blue, which, being blended together, are
considered to be an emblem of union, calculated
to remind the companions that the harmony and
unanimity of the Chapter should be their constant
aim. And as the glorious sun at its meridian
height dispels the mists and clouds which obscure
the horizon, so may their exertions tend to dispel
the gloom of jealousy and discord whenever they
may begin to appear.

Crimson is an emblem of imperial dignity, and
reminds us of the paternal concern which the
Principals ought ever to feel for the welfare of
the Chapter, and of the fervency and zeal with
which they should endeavour to promote its
prosperity.

'

CHAPTER II.

THE SECOND DIVISION OF THE PRIMITIVE RITUAL.

THIS part recounts the loss and recovery of the Sacred Word, but the legend is very differently arranged from that which was practised in the English Grand Lodge, although referring to the self-same event. Here the Senior Warden, who was formerly absent, takes his position in the west. The candidates now proceeded towards the east, and addressed the R. W. Master thus :— " Sire, our Most Worshipful Grand Master, Hiram, King of Tyre, having now arrived, we earnestly implore that you will confer upon us the high and sublime mysteries of a Geometrick Master Mason." The R. W. Master, casting his eyes towards the south, exclaimed : " The Chair in the south is vacant. Where is our worthy Grand Master, H. A. B. ? " One of the Brethren replied : " Sire, when we retired from labour to refreshment, at High Meridian, he remained behind. It is his custom to offer up his devotions at this hour to Him Whose name be exalted for ever. He may yet be at his devotions." The R. W. Master refusing to proceed

in his absence, the conducting Brother offered to
search for him about the precincts of the
Temple, &c.

After certain ceremonies, which I do not think
it expedient to describe, the Brethren made their
report. Then followed a representation of the
Arch,[1] and the recovery of the lost Word. The
R. W. Master then told the candidates that " We
permitted our lamented Brother, after casting the
two Pillars of the Porch, to engrave the mysterious

Word upon a plate of gold within the cabalistic
figure of our signet, and to wear it as a mark of

---

[1] "The vault or cavern here referred to, according to the
Ancients, was a place within the Sanctum Sanctorum. Solomon
had a deep cave dug underground, with many intricacies, over
which he fixed a stone, wherein he put the Ark and Cherubim.
They say he did this because, by the Holy Spirit foreseeing that
the Temple would be destroyed, he therefore made a secret
place where the Ark might be kept, so that its sanctity might
not be profaned by heathen hands ; and they are of opinion
that subsequently Josiah secreted therein the Ark of the Covenant."—*Manasseh Ben Israel, Concil.*, vol. ii. p. 75.

our royal favour and good will, and I have no doubt but it is still in his possession." Then followed the ceremony of finding the medal, which exhibited a double triangle enclosed within a circle, and the Tetragrammaton in the centre.[2] The medal was then placed upon the Holy Bible instead of the Square and Compasses, and when the Brethren resumed their seats, they were thus addressed by the R. W. Master:—

"Brethren, we are peculiarly fortunate in the recovery of this jewel, containing the mysterious Word, which would otherwise have been irrecoverably lost. If it had fallen into improper hands, they might have prized it for its metallic value, but they would not have understood its symbolical worth. These four letters compose the Tetragrammaton,[3] or sacred name of the

---

[2] A Masonic tradition of the period about which we are speaking taught the brethren that "it was the Sacred Word which expelled our erring parents from Paradise; which appeared in terror at the universal deluge; and on several occasions manifested itself to the patriarchs Abraham, Isaac, and Jacob, and also to Moses at the burning bush; after which it assumed a permanent form, and dwelt in the cloudy pillar as the image of the glory of God. This appearance was no other than the Tetragrammaton, which is so highly celebrated in many of the higher degrees of Masonry. This word conversed with Adam in Paradise, and is there called the Voice of God, which is nothing else than Jesus Christ the Messiah, that taketh away the sins of the world."

[3] An infidel writer in the United States gives the following account of this transaction, which, as might have been expected, was equally inaccurate both in doctrine and in fact. "The three Grand Masters, at the building of the Temple, entered into a solemn agreement not to confer the Master's degree

only true and living God. He, in His mercy,
condescended to reveal this name unto Enoch, to
Jacob, and to Moses, and it has descended to us
through Boaz, Obed, and Jesse, even by the lips
of our father David, of ever blessed memory.
Fearing, therefore, that this most precious name
should be lost to the world, and to our people in
particular, we did, in solemn convocation, communicate it to our royal friend, Hiram, King of
Tyre, and also to our departed Grand Master,
H. A. B.

"To the ends of the earth we were anxious that
His holy name should be carried, and to unborn

until the Temple should be completed; that all three must
necessarily be present when it should be conferred; and if
either of them should be taken away by death, prior to the
finishing of the Temple, the Master's Word would be lost.
After this arrangement, lest the knowledge of the arts and
sciences should be lost, they agreed to build a secret vault,
leading from Solomon's most retired apartment, a due west
course, and ending under the sanctum sanctorum of the Temple,
which they divided into nine separate arches. The ninth arch
was to be a place, not only for holding the Grand Council, but
also for a deposit of a true copy of all those things which were
contained in the Oracle above. After the ninth arch was completed, the three Grand 'Masters deposited therein all those
things which were considered important to the Craft. Before
the Temple was finished an accident occurred, which caused
the death of one of the Grand Masters, and consequently the
Master's Word was lost. The two remaining Grand Masters,
being willing to do all in their power to preserve the SACRED
WORD, as they could not now communicate it, agreed to place
it in the secret. vault, that if the other treasures were ever
brought to light, the Word might also be discovered." Fellows's
Inquiry into the Origin, History, and Purport of Freemasonry,"
p. 308.

generations of men for ever. What indeed could be more appropriate as a gift to those who assisted in erecting a House to His glory than the true name of the Great Creator, as a name revealed by Himself.[4]

"We write it in such a manner that no one can pronounce it except he receives it from human lips. That the high majesty of this most sacred word might not be profaned, behold how our lamented Grand Master preserved it at the cost, &c. &c. May this be an example to you, that at the great day you may be found to have, in like manner, preserved the Word of God in your souls inviolable and incorrupt. And that you may for ever bear in mind the sad scene you have just witnessed, let me exhort you to humble yourselves to the final condition of mortality, that you may be raised on the SIX points of fellowship, and entrusted with the mysterious secrets of a Geometrick Master Mason."

The six points of fellowship were then explained, the candidates invested, and the ceremony concluded with the following address, which was called a lecture :—

"Brethren, seeing that you are now clothed, it is

---

[4] The names revealed by the Most High to Moses were eleven in number, as follows : — 1. JEHOVAH. 2. EL, *strong and mighty*. 3. RACHUM, *merciful*. 4. CHANNUN, *gracious*. 5. EREOH APPAYM, *long-suffering*. 6. RAB, *great and mighty*. 7. CHESED, *bountiful*. 8. EMETH, *truth*. 9. NOTSER CHESED, *bountifulness*. 10. NOSEAVON, *the Redeemer*. 11. POKEDAVON, *retributive justice.—*See Exod. xxxiv. 6, 7.

necessary that you should have tools to work with. I will therefore present you with the working tools of a Master Mason, which are, every one of them, implements of Masonry, and especially the trowel. After the stones intended for a building have been hewn and properly squared, the trowel is used by operative Masons for uniting them together by means of cement. As Apprentices, you were employed in hewing; as Fellowcrafts, in adjusting and squaring; and now, as Master Masons, you will unite brother to brother by the cement of brotherly love, so that peace and concord may characterize all·your labours in this world, and earn for you a place in the eternal habitations of the next, where the everlasting Father of Love will reign for ever and ever.

"You are also, my Brethren, entitled, as Master Masons, to the use of an alphabet;[5] which our venerable Grand Master, H. A. B., employed in communicating with King Solomon, of Jerusalem, and King Hiram, of Tyre. It is geome-

---

[5] A writer of the last century informs us that a square, its portions, and the different positions into which those portions may be placed, with the aid of the dot, will form an alphabet of twenty-four letters, without the use of a quarter or single side, such as the Roman I. This is the secret alphabet of Masonry. It is very probable that the circle, triangle, and square, their divisions, and the varied positions of those divisions, first gave the idea of letters and an alphabet. The Egyptian letters are plainly of this character. One of the Greek letters is a triangle. The circle is common in almost all alphabets; the square in many, and the united divisions of both in all.

trick in its character, and is therefore eminently useful to Master Masons in general. By means of two squares and a mallet,[6] a Brother may make

[6] This was effected by the agency of the Masonic cypher, which consists of simple squares and angles; although I cannot think that two squares would furnish sufficient machinery for the purpose, unless one of them had a joint at the angle, to reduce the two limbs to one when necessary. A square, two 24-inch gauges, and the gavel or mallet appear to be the most efficient implements. But although Dermott boasted that the secret was known only to a few intelligent members of his own schism, yet it is quite evident that he himself learnt it on the Continent, where it was used by the Craft long before the time when he flourished; and it had been promulgated a hundred years earlier by the Marquis of Worcester, in the following words :—" A method by which, at a window, as far as the eye can discover black from white, a man may hold intercourse with his correspondent, without noise made or notice taken ; being according to occasion given or means afforded *ex re nata*, and no need of provision beforehand ; though much better if foreseen and course taken by mutual consent of parties, and may be carried on by night as well as by day, though as dark as pitch is black."

I subjoin a few of the most usual cyphers—

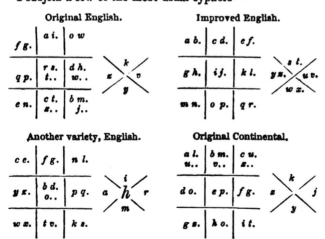

the whole alphabet, and silently convey his ideas
to another at any convenient distance.[7] That
this geometrick alphabet may be easily learned
and remembered, I will now entrust you with the
key thereof, which is as follows :—

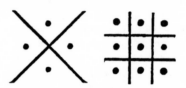

"This degree, as you have seen, was instituted,
by King Solomon, immediately after the dedica-

Improved Continental.			United States.		
a b.	c d.	e f.	a n.	b o.	c p.
g h.	i l.	m n.	d g.	e r.	f s.
o p.	q r.	s t.	g t.	h u.	i v.

This note has been extracted from an unpublished manuscript by the author of the present work, on the "Discrepancies
of Freemasonry," as they were discussed and settled at a
private convention holden at Grimsby, in the year 1825, in the
presence of Brothers Dr. Oliver, Peter Gilkes, and several
provincial celebrities, together with an accomplished foreign
Mason, where this and numerous other Masonic difficulties
were critically investigated.

[7] The author of the Freemason's Lexicon calls it an "ancient
cypher"; but this is a mistake, equally with the antiquity of its
origin. His words are :—"There is a very ancient cypher
extant amongst Masons, taken from the square and triangle,
which is called the Ammonian writing of the ancient Egyptian
priests. In the year 1808, Bro. J. G. Bruman, Director of the
Academy of Commerce, and Professor of the Mathematics at
Mannheim, published a programme of a pangraphia or uni-

tion of the Temple at Jerusalem, as a reward to the several expert and faithful Craftsmen who had laboured diligently and perseveringly in its erection. It was a reward not only to the Israelites, but also to those Tyrians who had renounced idolatry. His object in entrusting them with the great and mysterious name of the Almighty was that which Malachi afterwards prophesied would come to pass in time, that from the rising of the sun even to the going down of the same the Name of Jehovah would be great among the Gentiles, but the time was not yet come. The Assyrians invaded Tyre and destroyed it; the sacred name was corrupted, and in a mutilated form was soon after given to the idols of the Gentiles. When the Jews found this to be the case, they left off pronouncing it, and in process of time the true Name was lost to the Jewish people and nation. How it was recovered, and who restored it unto us, I must leave St. John the Evangelist to inform you by his Epistle to the Brethren at Ephesus,[8]

versal system of writing, and at the same time an arithmetical cryptographic, which was to be extremely useful in Freemasonry; but so far as we know this work has never appeared. The inquiring brother may profitably consult my Essay on the Masonic Cypher, in Vol. I. of the 'Golden Remains.'"

[8] Almost all the Apocryphal Gospels, Epistles, &c., may be traced generally to the early sect of the Docetæ, a branch of the Gnostics, the introducers of the mystic philosophy into Christianity, and in particular to a certain Leucius, said to have been a disciple of St. John, and who opposed these forgeries to the genuine writings of the Apostles, with the view of supporting the peculiar tenets of the sect, viz., that light and darkness, spirit and matter, are coeternally and coequally

which King Godefroy discovered among the Christian Brethren at Jerusalem, and which has come down to us faithfully preserved even unto this day."

opposed in hostility, &c. See more of this in Lord Lindsay's "Christian Mythology," x.

CHAPTER III.

THE TESTIMONY OF ST. JOHN THE EVANGELIST.

THE lecture concluded with the following address, supposed to have been pronounced by St. John to the Brethren at Ephesus, about the year of our Lord 98:—"Dearly beloved,—Now concerning the mysteries which have been revealed to us, it was on this wise. In those days, while the Temple was yet standing, it came to pass that the scribes and chief priests of the Jews heard of the wonderful things which were done by Jesus, and fearing him, they tried to explain them away as works done by Beelzebub. And Jesus, knowing their thoughts, said unto them:—'Every kingdom divided against itself shall be made desolate; if, therefore, Satan cast out Satan, he is divided against himself; how then shall his kingdom stand?'

"On hearing these words they were troubled, and answering, said unto Him:—'If the works done by Thee proceed from God, give unto us a sign from heaven whereby we may have testimony thereof.' And they proposed unto Him the true pronunciation of the quadriliteral word יהוה,

which composes the great Name that was revealed
to Moses, and which the Jews had lost during
their captivity under Nebuchadnezzar; for the
priests had substituted the name ADONAI, lest
the Gentiles should give this great Name to their
impotent gods.   And the chief priests said unto
Jesus:—' This great Name being lost to our people
and nation, no other person can restore it unto us
except the Messias himself.   If, therefore, thou
canst pronounce to us, by the power of Jehovah,
his most holy Name, we shall know certainly that
thou art he whom we look for, and not another.'
But Jesus turned away from them, saying :—' A
wicked and adulterous generation seeketh after a
sign, and a sign shall not be given unto it, save
and except the sign of the prophet Jonas.'

   " And he went out and departed from the
Temple.   But his disciples followed him, and
besought him, saying :—' Teach thou unto us the
forgotten Name of the Almighty, and the
mysteries thereof.'   Then taking Peter, James,
and John, he brought them up into a high mountain apart, and kneeling upon his knees, he
began to pray, when lo ! there appeared unto them
Moses the Lawgiver, unto whom Jehovah first
vouchsafed to reveal his holy Name, and whose
sepulchre no man knoweth to this day ; and likewise Elias, who was taken up to heaven in a
whirlwind of fire, and was the prototype of St.
John the Baptist.   And the face of Jesus did
shine as the sun, having also many great horns
of light.   And turning himself about, he per-

ceived that his disciples had fallen upon their faces in very great fear; so, coming to them, he raised them up from the earth and revealed unto them that great and glorious Name, Moses and Elias bearing testimony to his power over the living and the dead, and over things past, present, and to come. Here Jesus interpreted to them this most holy Name [IA—Ω—YA], signifying EVER-LASTING FATHER OF LOVE,[1] charging them likewise that they should tell no man what they had seen and heard upon the mount until after his resurrection.

"Now behold, fear came even yet more upon the disciples, and they trembled with exceeding great terror, for they had heard some of the mysteries of Jehovah; but Jesus comforted them, saying:—'Fear not, for from henceforth, in my Name, ye shall heal all manner of diseases and

---

[1] To the same effect we find the following passage in the Catholic Epistle of St. Barnabas : — "Understand, therefore, children, these things more fully, that Abraham, who was the first that brought in circumcision, looking forward in the spirit to Jesus, circumcised, having received *the mystery of Three Letters.* For the Scripture says that Abraham circumcised three hundred and eighteen men of his house. But what, therefore, was the mystery that was made known unto him ! Mark, first, the *eighteen,* and next the *three hundred.* For the numeral letters of *ten* and *eight* are I H. And these denote Jesus. And because the Cross was that by which we were to find grace, therefore he adds *three hundred,* the note of which is T, the figure of his cross. Wherefore by two letters he signified Jesus, and by the third his cross [I 廾]. He who has put the engrafted gift of his doctrine within us, knows that I never taught to any one a more certain truth. But I trust that ye are worthy of it."

raise the dead, yea, and cast out devils. As he
spake these words a shining cloud overshadowed
them, and a voice came out of the brightness,
saying :—' This is my beloved Son, hear ye him.'
And descending from the mount, they pondered
upon these things, but until his resurrection they
revealed them not to any one. Fervently then,
dearly beloved brethren, love one another, abiding
in the truth always."

Such was the first outline of the Royal Arch,
as a completion of the Third Degree, evidently
introduced into the Order of Freemasonry as
an exemplification of Protestant Christianity,
although the plan was subsequently extended by
the addition of the cavern and its mysterious contents, when the second part of the above ceremonies was placed under the government of a
Chapter, and dignified with the appellation of a
Fourth Degree. And the lecture, even when
introduced into our Grand Lodge by Brother
Dunckerley, in 1776, still retained a reference both
to Craft Masonry and Christianity, although the
pseudo Epistle of St. John was discarded.

CHAPTER IV.

THE EXCELLENT AND SUPER EXCELLENT DEGREES.

THE original identification of Craft with Royal Arch Masonry clearly appears from the preceding facts and arguments, but many learned brethren entertain grave doubts whether, under the present arrangement, any tangible connection between them can be fairly established. The Grand Lodges on the Continent of Europe, in the United States, in Ireland, and perhaps Scotland, pronounce the Royal Arch to be the seventh step or grade (and our own Floor Cloth ascends into the Chapter by seven steps),[1] separate and distinct from the symbolical degrees, the three grades of Past Master, Excellent and Super Excellent, being originally interposed between the Master Mason and the Royal Arch.

This arrangement is not now uniformly observed, for in some cases the intermediate steps

[1] The access to the Chapter by seven steps or degrees was a subsequent arrangement, and was probably the work of Michael Hayes, a Jew, about 1780 (Clavel says 1777), who introduced the degree into the United States along with other Masonic novelties.

vary. In the New World they are Mark, Past,
and Most Excellent Masters. In the best rituals
used by our Scottish Brethren the degree of
Excellent Master (comprehending three steps)
was supposed to be given at Babylon as a test, in
order to prevent mere Master Masons from par-
taking in the privilege of building a second
temple, except those to whom Cyrus gave per-
mission to return to Jerusalem for that purpose.
It was therefore a temporary degree, but during
the building an incident occurred on which the
Royal Arch was founded, and hence the Scotch
Masons use the degree of Excellent as an introduction to the Royal Arch. Indeed, they consider both to be temporary degrees, instituted for
a particular purpose, and not cosmopolite, like
true Masonry.

"I am induced to believe," says Brother Cole,
in his "Masonic Library," "that the founders of
this degree divided its secrets or ceremonies into
seven grades. It was incumbent upon them to
move slowly and to manage the subjects with
which they had to deal with much caution, for
fear of a disclosure. Besides, seven steps seem
necessary to complete the rounds of the holy
Royal Arch, the grand desideratum of Masonry."

It is quite clear, however, from the preceding
sketch, that the founders of the Order had no con-
ception of any such number of degrees; for their
own regulations distinctly specify, after the last
part had been severed from the Third Degree and
elevated to the dignity of a separate and inde-

pendent Order, that the candidate, being recommended by his Lodge, and found "well qualified
in the several degrees of Apprentice, Fellowcraft,
and Master Mason, and having passed the Chair,
was eligible to be admitted to the Supreme Degree
of an Excellent Royal Arch Mason." In the
Ahiman Rezon the Royal Arch is pronounced to
be the Fourth Degree (p. 113), and might occur
about the year 1744, because Brother D'Assigney,
in that year, says :—" Some of the Fraternity have
expressed their uneasiness at the Royal Arch being
kept a secret from them, since they had already
passed through the usual degrees of probation ; but
I cannot help being of opinion that they have no
right to any such benefit until they make a
proper application, and are received with due
formality as having passed the Chair and given
undeniable proofs of their skill."

The Excellent and Super Excellent Degrees
were conferred in Lodges governed by a Master
and Wardens, representing Moses, Aaron, and
Hur, and referred to the deliverance from Egyptian
bondage, the wanderings in the wilderness, and the
passage over the river Jordan into the Promised
Land. The rituals varied considerably in different
Lodges, although they usually bore a typical
reference to the legation of Moses, as will appear
from the following extracts.

In the first of these degrees, which is only preparatory, the candidate was furnished with a rod,
and with that instrument the reports were made,
in allusion to the action of Moses when he

stretched out his arms and smote the Red Sea three times, so that the Children of Israel went through as on dry ground, and Pharaoh and his host were drowned in their attempt to follow them. He then claimed admission to the Excellent Degree, by virtue of having passed through the three preliminary degrees of Craft Masonry, and being "impressed with a sincere wish and desire to participate in the privileges of this degree, humbly prays that his petition may be accepted." The petition was granted and he was admitted accordingly, and after the ceremonies were closed, he became, as it was technically termed, " a follower of Moses." [2]

[2] I have received many letters, in the course of my life, from different parts of the world, concerning the technical appellations by which the progress through the several orders and degrees in Masonry (so called) are distinguished. It may be useful, therefore, to insert the information here, as I may probably not be furnished with another opportunity. The E.A.P. is *initiated* in a Lodge, the Fellowcraft *passed*, and the Master Mason *raised;* the Mark Master *congratulated*, the Past Master *presided*, the Most Excellent Master *acknowledged and received*, and the Royal Arch Mason *exalted* in a Chapter. The American order of High Priesthood is called a *Convention*, and the candidate is said to be *anointed*. And further, an assembly of Knights Templars is called an *Encampment;* of Knights of the Christian Mark, a *Council;* of Illustrious Knights, a *Conclave;* of Knights of the East and West, a *Grand Council;* of Rose-Croix, a *Sovereign Chapter;* of Chevaliers K. H., an *Areopagus;* of Grand Inquisitor and Commander, a *Sovereign Tribunal;* of Princes of the Royal Secret, a *Consistory;* and of Grand Inspectors General, a *Convocation.* This explanation may be generally satisfactory, although slight variations occur under different systems in various parts of the world.

The Lecture, or Catechism, has but a single Section, besides the ceremony of admission, from which I subjoin a few brief particulars.

"Will you inform me in what manner the three candlesticks were placed upon the table? They were placed in a direct line, one behind the other, from east to west, two of them only being lighted.—Why did they appear in that form? They allude to that happy period when the Children of Israel passed through the Red Sea in their journey to the Promised Land. The two lighted candles symbolize the pillar of fire that lighted them through the sea; and also represent the two great lights, Moses and Aaron, that conducted them safely across. The extinguished candle represents the pillar of a cloud which covered the Egyptian army with darkness, and proved their utter overthrow.

"What do we understand by the Rod of Moses? The metaphor is taken from the custom of shepherds, who carry a rod to drive their sheep into green pastures, and the crook at the end of it is to catch them; and it reminds us of the true shepherd, Jesus Christ, according to the expression of our Grand Master David:—'Thy rod and Thy staff comforted me.'—What is the meaning of Aaron's rod blossoming and bearing fruit? It is intended to show how quickly those who are called by grace should blossom and bear heavenly fruit, and become faithful watchmen and seers of the night.

"Why is Christ called the foundation-stone of

His Church ?   He being the precious Stone taken
out of God's eternal rock, unto which the Church
and all its members are united by the cement of
faith and love.—How do we discover that union ?
It is undiscernible by carnal eyes.   Like the
stones of the typical temple, which were so admi-
rably laid and united that the joints could not
be perceived, and it appeared to be constructed
of one entire stone.   Neither can we discern
these things until we are enlightened by the Grace
of God."

The degree of Super Excellent is governed by
the same officers as the former, Moses being
distinguished by a broad green sash, while those
of Aaron and Hur were white.   Two rods in
saltire were placed behind the chairs of the members present.   The three lights were in a right
line, with a single light at a distance, by which
sat Joshua attired in a crimson sash, with the
Bible and Sword in front, as Captain of the Lord's
Host.   The *Report* alludes to that period of time
when Moses struck the rock with his rod in the
desert of Zin, out of which there came an abun-
dance of water to supply the wants of the children
of Israel, and caused their murmurings to cease.
After some preliminary ceremonies the Master
thus addresses the candidate :—

" Excellent Brother, the signs and tokens of the
Super Excellent degree were known to that inspired man, Moses, who was selected from amongst
thousands of his brethren, by the Most High, to
bring His chosen people out of bondage, and to

publish His laws, not only to them, but to the whole world. After the deliverance, Moses caused a Tent or Tabernacle to be erected in the wilderness, under the immediate direction of God himself; and being sensible that he could not remain with them for ever, He transmitted to others the signs, tokens, laws, and commands of the Lord their God; and in like manner I will now intrust you with the secrets, signs, and tokens of this Super Excellent Order."

This degree is more comprehensive than the former, and the lecture consists of three sections, from which I extract the following specimens for the purpose of pointing out its tendency:—"Excellent Brother, when you first came into a Lodge of Super Excellent Masons, what principally struck your attention? The form in which the four lights were placed.—Be kind enough to inform me what those situations were? The principal lights were placed in an horizontal line; and at a distance I saw a smaller light, with the Bible and Sword.—Whom do the three great lights represent? They are the representatives of Moses, Aaron, and Hur.—Give me a reason for this? Because Moses was chosen to bring the Lord's peculiar people out of their Egyptian bondage; Aaron was appointed to be His spokesman, and Hur His chief priest.—There is another reason which I will thank you to specify? When the Israelites were journeying into the land of promise, the Amalekites refused them a passage through their dominions; they therefore collected their armies and encamped in the valley of Rephidim. Moses, Aaron, and Hur, previous to the battle, went to the top of a hill near the place where it was to be fought; for it had been divinely communicated to Moses, that the rod with which he smote the Red Sea should be a safeguard to him and all Israel, so long as they observed His laws, and kept His commandments. And when the battle had begun, with great fury on both sides, Moses lifted up his hands, which held the miraculous rod, and then the Israelites prevailed. But when, through weariness, he let his hands drop, the Amalekites prevailed. On which Aaron and Hur placed themselves on each side of Moses, and supported his arms in a continued state of elevation. The Israelites in consequence of this prevailed, and put to flight the whole army of their enemies. Thus the Lord manifested His gracious power and protection to Moses, as He had promised even before they left the house of bondage.

"What did the Light at a distance signify? It represented Joshua, the chosen servant of the Lord, who that day was at the bottom of the hill with the armies of Israel, and there discomfited the Amalekites with a high hand, according to the promise of the Most High, who fought that day for Israel, and called the place Jehovah Nissi."

It may be unnecessary to give any further extracts from this Lecture, which includes a minute description of the Tabernacle and its appendages, the Oracle, the Ark and Mercy Seat, and the

Cloudy Pillar; together with the passage of the river Jordan, the demolition of Jericho, and a number of reasons why Moses was a type of Christ; and closes with this admonition :—"We learn that the Israelites were not permitted to enter the Promised Land till after the death of Moses; and in like manner our Saviour opened the kingdom of heaven to all believers, and promised another Comforter, who could not come till He had ascended into Heaven. Shortly afterwards that Comforter was vouchsafed, in the form of cloven tongues of fire resting on the heads of His disciples, and enabling them to speak in all tongues, and to understand all languages. Therefore, let us, Super Excellent Masons, give all glory and praise to God our Saviour, the true Comforter, both now and for evermore."

CHAPTER V.

CRAFT MASONRY AND THE ROYAL ARCH.

In the Articles of Union it is distinctly provided that the Royal Arch shall be considered as a completion of the Third Degree; and we have already seen that, at its original promulgation, it formed an essential part of that degree. In order to reduce this principle to practice, and to make it permanently understood, it is ordained in the General Regulations, as a perpetual and unalterable Landmark, that "the Grand Master of the Fraternity shall be the First Grand Principal, if a Royal Arch Mason. The Deputy Grand Master, if a Royal Arch Mason, is to be the Second Grand Principal; the Grand Secretary is to be the Grand Scribe E.; and the Grand Treasurer and Registrar of the Craft to occupy the same offices in the Grand Chapter.[1]"

[1] And it is also impressed on the candidate, at his exaltation by the First Principal, in these words:—"Allow me to congratulate you on your admission into the sublime and exalted degree of a Royal Arch Mason, which is at once the foundation and copestone of the whole Masonic structure. You may perhaps conceive that you have received this day a Fourth Degree of Freemasonry, but such is not the case: it is only the completion of that of a Master Mason."

Those Grand Lodges which have disconnected the Royal Arch from the Third Degree of Craft Masonry profess to be actuated by these considerations:—1. because it now contains no reference to the transactions of the Third Degree; 2. it embraces a different series of facts; 3. includes a different period of time; and 4. celebrates the building of another edifice, although situated on the self-same spot of ground which forms the consecrated floor of our Craft Lodges. In a word, they contend that the Royal Arch contains nothing in common with Symbolical Masonry, except the SACRED NAME, which was originally attached to the Third Degree, and in one of its most ancient lectures, used, or at least sanctioned, by Sir C. Wren, when Grand Master, and consequently many years before the Royal Arch was fabricated. The Landmark is thus expressed :—"Whence come you ? From the East.—Whither going ? To the West.—For what purpose? To seek for that which was lost, *but is now found.*—What is that which was lost, and is now found? THE MASTER MASON'S WORD."

I am no way concerned in reconciling the anomalies of the Royal Arch, because I consider it to be incidental to ancient Masonry only as the present depository of this alienated Word. A Lodge, however, may exist without the addition of a Chapter; and even where a Chapter does exist, its Charter may be forfeited without compromising the Lodge. The discrepancies of the Royal Arch, however, could scarcely be rectified without an entire reconstruction; or, in other words, without the formation of a new degree. Indeed, the last revision of the Royal Arch is essentially different from the ritual which was manufactured by the seceding Brethren, and introduced by Dunckerley, with certain modifications, into the London Grand Lodge. I have, amongst my Masonic papers, a corrected copy of his entire lecture; which, it must be confessed, abounds in errors and anachronisms for want of the intervening links. It contains four sections, and about a hundred questions and answers. The first two sections contain the ceremony of Exaltation; the third refers to the Grand, Sacred, and Royal Lodges; and the fourth to the building of the Second Temple. The subjoined extracts will show the connection which existed between Craft Masonry and the Royal Arch at the period when that celebrated Freemason flourished.

"How did you obtain that Word? By having been made a true and lawful Entered Apprentice; passed and raised to the sublime degree of a Master Mason, according to King Solomon's directions. I was then appointed Master of a Lodge; and having served that office with freedom, fervency, and zeal, as a reward for my fidelity, I was entrusted with the Word, which none but a Past Master, or a Master regularly placed in the Chair, ought to know.—What does that Word signify? An Excellent Mason or Master of Science."

*   *   *   *   *

" How long was Solomon's Temple in building?
Seven years and six months.—How was it possible
so stupendous a building could have been erected
in so short a time, when we read that the Temple
of Diana at Ephesus—a far inferior edifice—took
two hundred years in its completion? Because
T. G. A. O. T. U., in His infinite wisdom, endued
King Solomon and his abettors with sufficient
talent for the purpose.—How many Master Masons
were present at the building? Three thousand
six hundred.—What proof have you of that?
There were three thousand six hundred pure
marble pillars in the Temple, and a pillar set up
in honour of each of the two Royal Grand Masters, with the name of each inscribed thereon;
but there was no pillar found with the name of
the third Grand Master, until the descent of the
Royal Arch.—How were the workmen paid? In
the usual places and in the accustomed manner.—
Where was the foundation-stone laid? In the
north-east corner. It was a block of pure white
marble, without speck or stain, and alluded to the
chief corner stone on which the Christian Church
was built; which, although rejected by the Elders,
afterwards became the head-stone in the corner.—
What part of the temple was first finished? The
Royal Arch.—Why was it called Royal? Because
there were two royal persons concerned, who
chose to become operative masons for the purpose
of erecting it, as a depository for the Grand and
Sublime Word."

At the close of this chapter it may be added,

that there exist among the Fraternity, even in
England, conflicting opinions on many subjects
connected with Craft Masonry and its radiating
branches.   Nor is it strange that it should be so.
Men's habits of thinking are so different, and they
see the same objects from such various points
of view, that we do not wonder to find adverse
opinions on the most trifling propositions.   The
colour of the cameleon is determined according to
the medium through which it is seen.   To one it
appears black, to another white, to a third green,
and to a fourth red or blue.   And there are so
many unexplained anomalies in Freemasonry,
that a perfect agreement on every subject is
morally impossible.   Nor is it necessary.   So long
as the Fraternity are unanimous on the identity
of its broad outline, and the ancient Landmarks
are preserved in their integrity, discordant opinions
on minor points will be rather beneficial than
otherwise ; inasmuch as truth is elicited by the
process of ratiocination, in the same manner as
metals receive their finest polish by a regulated
series of successful operations in the hands of
skilful workmen.

CHAPTER VI.

THE SEAL OF SOLOMON.

IT was an observation of Sir H. Davy, that "men of genius in former times have often languished in obscurity, not because their merits were neglected, but because they were not understood. This, however, can scarcely happen in the present day, in which all sources of useful information are laid open, and in which unparalleled exertions have been made in the higher classes of society to diffuse useful improvement, and to promote all objects of inquiry which can benefit or enlighten the public. There are other uses, still greater uses, resulting from the communication of general and popular science. By means of it vulgar errors and common prejudices are constantly diminished. It offers new topics for conversation, and for an active exercise of the understanding; and in cities it assists the cause of morality and religion, by preventing the increase of gross luxury and indulgence in vicious dissipation. Man is designed for an active being, and his spirit, ever restless, if not employed upon worthy and dignified objects, will often rather engage in mean and low pursuits than suffer the tedious and listless feelings connected with indolence; and knowledge is no less necessary in strengthening the mind, than in preserving the purity of the affections and the heart."

These are sentiments which I have long applied to the science of Freemasonry; and have accordingly endeavoured to illustrate the science and philosophy of the Order, that its super-eminent merits may be open to public examination. Whether the institution has derived any benefit from my exertions, must be left to the decision of the Fraternity; and I am not without hope that the sentence will be favourable.

The first Book of Constitutions of the Royal Arch was issued by the Supreme Grand Chapter in 1786, the laws having been agreed to 10th May, 1782. I have made use of this as an authentic document, in the following pages, because I consider its evidence to be conclusive. The introductory address, from which I have quoted largely, points out the construction which our rulers of that period put upon "The Word," that it was intended "to convey to the mind some idea of Him by whom all things were made; even the Word mentioned by St. John, who was in the beginning with God, and was God; for all things were made by Him, and without Him was not anything made that was made; even T. G. A. O. T. U."

The first Grand Principal by whom the above-mentioned code was signed was John Allen, who was also the Grand Superintendent over the counties of Chester and Lancaster. His colleagues were Sir Herbert Mackworth, Bart., President of the Council; James Hesletine, and John Brookes, Esqrs., who held the great seal of the Order in commission, and were Inspectors General; Francis Const, Esq., Treasurer; and James Galloway, Thomas Dunckerley, Richard Garland, and John Allen, Esqrs., Provincial Superintendents; and with these were associated, all under the grand patronage of H.R.H. the Duke of Cumberland, Sir Peter Parker, Bart., Lieut.-General Rainsford, Thomas Preston, Esq., the Rev. John Frith, Bartholomew Ruspini, Esq., and other eminent Companions.

Throughout the entire system of Freemasonry, whether practised by Heathens, Jews, or Christians, as in successive ages we find it to have been, the MASON-WORD [1] always appears surrounded

---

[1] "How comes it that a doctrine so singular, and so utterly at variance with all the conceptions of uninstructed reason, as that of a Trinity in Unity, should have been from the beginning a fundamental religious tenet of every nation upon earth? The answer is—a WORD, a sacred, ineffable, triune NAME, showing forth the attributes of the Almighty, and faintly shadowing the afterwards revealed doctrine of the Trinity, was given to man at his creation, as the bond or type of union between the Spirit of God placed in man, and the spirit which created the body from dust. This Word was long preserved by man, but in process of time, in consequence of the increasing wickedness of the world in falling away from God, was lost. Can we pierce this mystery? To the Royal Arch Mason I would say—he who seeketh rightly shall find."—Bro. Chanter, in the *F. Q. R.*

G

with a peculiar mystery. Its various modifications, as it passed through the hands of those people by whom it was consecutively preserved, have been the theme of endless speculation; and there is no nation, kindred, or people, with whom it has not constituted a curious subject of inquiry. Even its pronunciation has been variously interpreted; and some have gone so far as to refrain altogether from using it, until, as it is now believed, the true pronunciation is irrecoverably lost.

The same thing is said to have happened amongst the Jews respecting the name of Jehovah. They were afraid the Heathen should get possession of it, and, therefore, in their copies of the Scriptures, they wrote it in the Samaritan characters instead of the Hebrew or Chaldee, that the adversary might not make an improper use of it; for they believed it capable of working miracles, and held that the wonders in Egypt were performed by Moses, in virtue of this name being engraven on his rod; and that any person, who knew the true pronunciation, would be able to do as much as he did. In like manner, the Heathen had names of their gods which it was not lawful to utter, lest nature should be subverted, and the earth dissolved.[2]

---

[2] The followers of Mahomet have a tradition that there is a secret name of the Deity which possesses wonderful properties, and that the only method of becoming acquainted with it is by being initiated into the mysteries of the Ism Abla. Lane has illustrated its power by an anecdote from the Koran. It appears that two rebel angels, called Haroot and Maroot, were believed to be confined in the subterranean caverns which exist amidst

From the above belief amongst the Jews, enforced by the consideration that the Shekinah actually delivered oracular responses to the high priest, the idea of attaching oracles to the heathen temples probably originated; and in all cases the power was supposed to result from a cabalistic use of the name of the deity; and these superstitions descended to the Mahometans and the Christians. It was commanded in the Jewish law, that sentences from the Scriptures should be inscribed on the door-posts of their dwellings; [a] and therefore the Jews had a custom of writing the Decalogue on a square piece of parchment, which they rolled up, and put into a case; and after inscribing *the name of God* within a circle on the outside, they affixed it to the door-posts of their houses, or private apartments, and considered it a talisman of safety.

It was probably from this custom that the prophet of Mecca recommended his followers, when they closed their doors at night, to repeat *the name of God*, which would render them

the ruins of Babylon, and there suspended by the feet for an indefinite length of time. They had been sent amongst mankind as examples, and had sinned, for which this punishment was inflicted on them. The celebrated Mujahid visited them under the guidance of a Jew, who particularly cautioned him not to mention the NAME OF GOD in their presence; but when he beheld them, like two mountains suspended upside down, he expressed his astonishment by uttering the forbidden NAME; on which the two angels became so violently agitated, that they almost broke the irons which confined them, and Mujahid and his guide fled in the utmost consternation.

[a] Deut. vi. 9.

impervious to the intrusion of evil genii. The
Arabs have some curious anecdotes respecting the
use that Solomon made of the sacred name. It
was engraven on a seal ring,[4] composed of brass
and iron mixed; by virtue of the former he commanded the good, and by the latter the evil genii.
His power over them was unlimited, and they
add, that it was by their aid that he built the
temple at Jerusalem.[5]   By pronouncing the

---

[4] According to the Talmud, it was Solomon's custom, while
he washed himself, to entrust his Signet, on which his kingdom
depended, with a concubine of his named Amina; one day,
therefore, when she had the ring in her custody, a devil, named
Sakhar, came to her in the shape of Solomon, and received the
ring from her; by virtue of which he became possessed of the
kingdom, and sat on the throne in the shape which he had
borrowed, making what alterations in the law he pleased;
Solomon, in the meantime, being changed in his outward appearance, and known to none of his subjects, was obliged to wander
about and beg alms for his subsistence; till at length, after the
space of forty days, the devil flew away, and threw the signet
into the sea: the signet was immediately swallowed by a fish,
which being taken and given to Solomon, he found the ring in
its belly, and having by this means recovered the kingdom, took
Sakhar, and tying a great stone to his neck, threw him into the
lake of Tiberias.

[5] The Mussulmans feign that David having laid the foundations of the temple of Jerusalem, which was to be in lieu of the
Tabernacle of Moses, when he died, left it to be finished by his
son Solomon; who employed the genii in the work;—that
Solomon, before the edifice was quite completed, perceiving his
end draw nigh, begged of God that his death might be concealed
from the genii till they had entirely finished it: that God therefore so ordered it, that Solomon died as he stood at his prayers,
leaning on his staff, which supported the body in that posture
a full year; and the genii, supposing him to be alive, continued
their work during that term; at the expiration whereof, the

Name, his minister Asaf transported the Queen of Sheba to his presence; and performed other wonderful works.

The magicians of our own country made a similar use of the sacred name of God. When one of them desired to practise his art, he put on his magical robes, accompanied by an invocation in this form :—" By the figurative mystery of this holy vestment, I will clothe me with the armour of salvation in the strength of ADONAI, to whom be glory and praise for ever." After other ceremonies, which are of no moment here, he invoked the spirits " by the strong and mighty NAME of JEHOVAH; by his holy name TETRAGRAMMATON, and by all the wonderful names and attributes, Dadai, Sillon, Paracletos, &c., &c." We have the authority of King James for saying, that in his time spirits were invoked by the use of " circles and *triangles, double and single*." And as with the Jews and Mahometans, the Christians of the middle ages were imbued with a firm belief that the name of God was a powerful protection from unclean spirits.[6]

Temple being perfectly completed, a worm, which had gotten into the staff, ate it through, and the corpse fell to the ground, and discovered the king's death. The Rabbins also tell us of a worm which assisted the workmen, its virtue being such as to cause the rocks and stones to fly in sunder. Our *ancient* brethren of the last century talked a great deal about this worm, which they called the *Insect Shermah,* and were so chary about its name and marvellous performances, that they carefully kept them a profound secret.

[6] The above charm ran in this form :—" In nomine Patris, et Filii, et Spiritus Sancti, Amen. + a + g + l + a +. TETRA-

The mystery which overshadows the WORD of
Freemasonry has always been replete with interest,
and constitutes the excitement that leads the
inquirer from one degree to another, till he is
rewarded by a participation in this ineffable
secret.   It is in vain that the oppugner of
Masonry affects to believe that we possess no
such claims on the attention, because he conscientiously feels that he is feigning an objection
which cannot be substantiated.   He envies our
knowledge, although prejudice prevents him from
sharing in the advantages it conveys.   It is in
vain that apostate Masons tell the world, that
they themselves were urged forward from step to
step, under the promise that this great secret
would be ultimately revealed, but which was
always evaded under one pretext or another.
The Brethren of the Order glory in the possession
of a secret which never has been, nor ever can be
revealed.   "It is as a strong tower; the righteous
runneth into it and is safe." [7]

GRAMMATON. + ALPHA + OMEGA. + A. Ω. + Primogenitus
+ Sapientia + Virtus. + JESUS NAZARENUS REX JUDEORUM.
+ Fili Domini. + Miserere mei. + Amen. + Matheus.
+ Marcus. + Lucas. + Johannes. + Mihi succurrite et
defendite. + Amen. +." The Abraxas of the Basilideans
partook of this nature. It was a gem or stone, with the word
Abraxas engraven on it, accompanied by curious designs of
natural or artificial objects. Montfaucon has given engravings
of several hundreds of them. Every individual who joined the
society of the Gnostics was presented with this gem, which was
supposed to secure the protection of the Deity to whom it was
dedicated, to avert calamity, and to convey health, prosperity,
and safety.   [7] Prov. xviii. 10.

At the establishment of the Royal Arch degree during the last century, a passage from the first chapter of St. John's Gospel was introduced, in which the LOGOS, or WORD, is pronounced to be T. G. A. O. T. U., or CHRIST, or GOD, on the authority of Holy Scripture; for JEHOVAH said, by the mouth of his prophet, " I have sworn by myself, and the WORD is gone out of my mouth in righteousness, and shall not return; that unto me every knee shall bow, and every tongue shall swear." [8] Now these very words are twice applied in the New Testament to Jesus Christ. St. Paul says,[9] " We shall all stand before the judgment seat of CHRIST; for it is written, As I live, saith the Lord, every knee shall bow to me, and every tongue shall confess." And again, more plainly; [10] " At the Name of Jesus every knee shall bow."

The passage above referred to, was used by the holy Evangelist to refute certain heterodox doctrines, which had been propounded by the Gnostics, to the effect that "the Supreme Deity first generated an only begotten Son, who again begat the Word, which was inferior to the first born. That Christ was inferior to the Word. That there were two Spirits distinct from Christ, the one called *Life*, and the other *Light;* and that the Creator, or the G. A. O. T. U., was a still lower spirit, called Demiurgus, who formed the world out of eternal matter." These absurdities

[8] Isa. xlv. 23.　　[9] Rom. xiv. 10, 11.　　[10] Phil. ii. 10.

were set at rest by the passage in question ; which was the beginning of his Gospel—"In the beginning was the WORD, and the Word was with God, and the WORD was GOD. All things were made by him; and without him was not anything made that was made. In him was *Life ;* and the Life was the *Light* of men. And the Light shineth in darkness, and the darkness comprehended it not."

CHAPTER VII.

A PRIMITIVE TRACING BOARD OF THE ROYAL ARCH.

I HAVE had the good fortune to meet with a very curious Floor Cloth of the Royal Arch degree, as it was practised in the Grand Lodge of England, at the period of its introduction into what was then denominated *modern* Masonry by Brother Dunckerley, which clearly illustrates the principles already enunciated. It is painted on silk (size 22 by 18 inches), and is the property of the St. Michael's Chapter No. 24, in the city of Chester, and was forwarded to me by my friend and brother, Willoughby, of Birkenhead. The Warrant for this Chapter is dated February 9th, 1781, and differs very little from the present form, except that it is dedicated to " the Almighty JAH ⌐⅃." It is signed by the three Principals, two Scribes, and three Sojourners, and also by three Inspectors General. An old jewel which belonged to this Chapter, has a mitre upon it, on which is inscribed HOLINESS TO THE LORD.

This ancient document I have thought of sufficient importance to present to my readers in a lithograph. Here we have an arch and keystone, the latter not drawn but remaining in its place. The sun darting its rays

obliquely into the arch, needs no explanation.
Upon an arched fillet in the centre are the words
EN APXH HN O ΛOΓOΣ; "In the beginning
was the Word;" and beneath, in the centre of
the floor-cloth, a broad circle containing the
interlaced triangles and a blaze of Light, to represent the mysterious Name or Word.[1] Below that,
in an inferior situation, on three fillets, are the
words, Solomon, King of Israel; Hiram, King of
Tyre; and Hiram, the widow's son, at length, in
the Hebrew character.   Several Masonic emblems
which were formerly attached to the third degree,
are disposed in order; viz., the golden candlestick,
the table of shew bread, the pot of manna and of
incense, Aaron's rod, &c., all of which were
appendages to the tabernacle, and typical of the
Christian dispensation.

Now, the very existence of these emblems in a
Royal Arch floor-cloth, to which degree they are
incongruous, and not in any respect applicable,
betrays the source from whence the degree was
drawn.   And hence it was that Brother Dunckerley, and others, who grafted the degree on to

---

[1] This mysterious Name or Word, called in many parts of the
sacred writings, "the Voice of God," is about our bed, and
about our path, and spieth out all our ways. King Solomon
tells us that he dwelleth in the thick darkness, because the Holy
of Holies in the Temple was perfectly dark, being enlightened
only by the Divine Shekinah, with whom darkness and light
are both alike. Freemasons, however, say that He dwells in
Light ineffable, because he is styled the Father of Lights; the
Light of the World; a Light to lighten the Gentiles; the Light
of Righteousness, and the Light of life.

modern Masonry, very judiciously restored them
to the third degree, whence they had been inconsiderately divorced, to the manifest injury of both;
and a copious explanation of them was incorporated into the third lecture, that the application
might be legitimatized, and their direct reference
permanently fixed into the degree, so that no
further doubt might exist about their true Masonic
reference. I place some stress upon this point,
because this primitive floor-cloth is an existing
fact which it would be difficult to overturn. I
am further inclined to think that the fabricators
of the Royal Arch intended it to be a Christian
degree,[2] not only for the above reasons, but
because they adopted the Christian emblems ✡
and ⊓ as its legitimate insignia. And I have in
my possession a fragment of an old Royal Arch
lecture, which contains the following passage :—

[2] The Christian tendency of the Order was embodied in the
Lodge Lectures by the worthies who resuscitated Freemasonry
in 1717, all of whom were Protestant Christians, though differing
on the subject of Church government. At that period the
Redeemer was officially denominated T. G. A. O. T. U.; and
Christianity pronounced, in the ancient Gothic Charges, to be
an unalterable Landmark of Masonry. The fraternity were
enjoined as a fundamental principle, to "believe in the Glorious
Architect of heaven and earth, and to practise the sacred duties
of Christian morality." And to render it unmistakeably clear
that this was truly the Masonic Name of the founder of our
religion, the revivers of masonry inserted in the Examination
which was compiled for the use of the Lodges, the following
interpretation of a certain Letter, which cannot by any possibility
be misunderstood. "What did that Letter denote? The Grand
Architect and Contriver of the Universe, or He that was taken
up to the topmost pinnacle of the holy Temple."

" A Royal Arch Chapter is called the Grand and
Royal Lodge, in verification of the prophecy of
Jacob, that the sceptre should not depart from
Judah, nor a lawgiver from between his feet
until SHILOH come." [3] And again,—" The three
Great Lights represent the Sublime Word in
three different points of view; but more particularly that superior light which shone forth in the
Gospel Revelation, when the mystery of the
Trinity was publicly displayed at the baptism
of Christ." [4] And in another place we have this
remarkable explanation :—" The reason why we
enter the Chapter upon the Holy Bible and the
interlacing equilateral triangles, refers to the
Roll of the Law which was found at the building
of the second temple. This roll represented the

---

[3] And the same passage still occurs in our Historical Lecture,
when the third Principal explains that " the kingly power was
not effaced until after the destruction of the City and Temple by
the Romans under Titus, in the year 70 of the present era ;
thus verifying the remarkable prophecy of Jacob delivered in
Egypt above a thousand years before—that the Sceptre should
not depart from Judah, nor a Lawgiver from between his feet
until SHILOH come."

[4] There is a MS. in the British Museum (Harl. Col. Vol.
1942), which professes to explain the ancient history and principles of Freemasonry, the original of which is dated in the 10th
century, and was written in Saxon during the reign of Athelstan.
It commences thus :—" The Almighty FATHER of Heaven, with
the Wisdom of his glorious SON, through the goodness of the
HOLY GHOST, Three persons in one Godhead, be with our
beginning, and give us grace to govern our lives that we may
come to his bliss that never shall have an end. Amen. Good
brethren and fellows ; our purpose is to tell you how, and in
what manner, this Craft of Masonry was first begun, &c."

Bible,[5] and the equilateral triangles the New Testament, or in other words, the Trinity in Unity." [6] And the Scroll commenced, according to an original formula of the Order, with the following passage :—

"In the beginning was the Word,
And the Word was with God,
And the Word was God." [7]

---

[5] In speaking of the Roll which was found by Hilkiah in the Temple, Dr. Clark inquires whether this was the autograph of Moses ? And answers—"It is very probable that it was, for in another place it is described as the Book of the law of the Lord by Moses. The Rabbins say that Ahaz, Manasseh, and Amon endeavoured to destroy all the copies of the law, and this only was saved by being *buried under a paving-stone.* It is scarcely reasonable, however, to suppose that this was the only copy of the Law that was found in Judea ; for even if we grant that Ahaz, Manasseh, and Amon had endeavoured to destroy all the books of the law, yet they could not possibly have succeeded so completely as to destroy the whole ! "

[6] Among the ancient Chinese characters, we find one resembling the Greek delta Δ, which was subsequently written 𠂇 , and signifies union, harmony, the chief good ; and, in a word, the union of three in one. The book *See-ki* says, "formerly the Emperor made a solemn sacrifice every three years to the spirit Trinity in Unity 𡗜 ⊟≡ — *chin, san y,* and refers to the eternity of the divine being. For they say, there is no Name which can designate him. He bears no similitude to any created thing. He is an image without form ; and a form without matter. His light is encompassed with darkness. If you look upwards you cannot see his beginning ; if you follow him you cannot discover his end.

[7] John i. 1. This is now a ered, and the first three verses of the first chapter of Genesis substituted. On the above passage, the learned Stanley Faber has this judicious remark :— " It is impossible not to perceive, in the exordium of the Gospel

Respecting this passage of Scripture, I have elsewhere stated that the early Christians considered it to be a formula in use from the most ancient times, and adopted by St. John, because it constituted an unanswerable argument in proof of the doctrine which he was anxious to establish, viz., the eternal divinity of Christ, and his identity with Jehovah, the creator of the world.   It is recorded by Philostorgius, and after him by Nicephorus, that at the clearing of the foundations on mount Moriah, when Julian the apostate commenced his insane attempt to rebuild the temple, a stone was taken up that covered the mouth of a deep vault sunk into the rock.   One of the workmen was let down by a rope fastened round his waist, and found some water at the bottom, out of which, in the centre of the vault, rose a pedestal on which lay a Roll or Book, wrapped up in a covering of fine linen.   Being drawn up, and the Roll unfolded, it was found to contain the Holy Scriptures, beginning with the words which are inscribed on the uppermost fillet in the old floor-cloth above referred to.[8]

according to St. John, a studied reference to the exordium which introduces the Mosaic Cosmogony. Each commences with the phrase, *In the beginning;* and in both places the phrase must obviously be understood in the same sense. The additional information given by St. John is, that while Moses simply states the Creator of the Universe to be God, the inspired Apostle further informs us, that all things were created or caused to subsist through the agency of the WORD OF GOD; so that without him, nothing that subsisted, had been caused to subsist."

[8] Philost. L. vii. c. 14.   Niceph. l. x. p. 76.

The true Name of God in every age of the world, amongst the patriarchs and Jews, was JEHOVAH. Moses said to the latter, "The Lord (Jehovah) God of your fathers hath sent me unto you. This is my Name for ever."[9] "And God himself," says Dr. Willet,[10] "Jehovah, Christ, the Mediator both of the Old and New Testament, was the giver of the law; and that it was he himself that talked with Moses, by these reasons it is made plain. 1. Because he is called Jehovah, which is the proper and essential Name of God. 2. Moses himself saith, Jehovah spake unto you out of the midst of the fire. And 3, because Origen saith, In the end of the world Jesus Christ became man; but before his manifestation in the flesh, he was the Mediator between God and man: and Calvin adds, "That there never was any intercourse between God and man, but by Jesus Christ."

David and Hosea make the same declaration. The former says, "Thy Name, O Lord (Jehovah), endureth for ever; and thy memorial, O Lord (Jehovah), throughout all generations;"[11] and the latter, "Even the Lord God of Hosts, Jehovah is his Name."[12] The Being spoken of in these passages is the same divine personage as Jesus, the founder of Christianity, pronounced by St. John to be T. G. A. O. T. U., or the Creator of

[9] Exod. iii. 15.
[11] Psalm cxxxv. 13.
[10] Hexapla, p. 802.
[12] Hosea xii. 5.

the world;" [13] which is confirmed by St. Paul—
"Thou Lord (Christ) in the beginning hast laid
the foundation of the earth; [14] which is but a
reiteration of what the Psalmist had already
affirmed of Jehovah—"Of old hast Thou (Jehovah)
laid the foundation of the earth." [15]   Again, the
prophet Zechariah had said—"I will dwell in the
midst of thee, said Jehovah;" [16] and "they shall
look on me (Jehovah) whom they have pierced;" [17]
both of which were applied expressly to the
Saviour of mankind by St. John—"The Word
was made flesh, and dwelt amongst us." [18]   And
"they shall look on him (Jesus Christ) whom
they pierced." [19]

[13] He who made the heavens and the earth is T. G. A. O. T.U.,
"at whose command," as it is expressed in our Exaltation
prayer, "the world burst forth from Chaos, and all created
matter had its birth." But the worlds were made by Christ ;
(John i. 1, 2.—Heb. i. 10—xi. 3.—Col. i. 15, 16, 17). The
Messiah of Scripture prophecy, and represented in Masonry by
"the union of Three Taus ᚼ which alludes to the Great
JEHOVAH, by whom the gloomy and unshapen masses were
changed into regular form and peaceful order." And therefore
Jesus Christ is T. G. A. O. T. U. Whence we are taught by
our Fiducial Sign, that "if we prostrate ourselves with our
faces to the earth, it is to implore the mercy of our Creator and
Judge ; relying with humble confidence on his most gracious
promises, by which alone we hope to pass through the Ark of
our Redemption into the mansions of our eternal bliss and glory,
and the presence of Him who is the Great I. A. U., the *Alpha*
and *Omega*, the beginning and the ending, the first and the
last." (From the Mystical Lecture of the Royal Arch.)

[14] Heb. i. 10.   [15] Psalm cii. 25.   [16] Zech. ii. 10.
[17] Zech. xii. 10.   [18] John i. 14.
[19] John xix. 37. See more of this in my "Apology for the
Freemasons," p. 20.

CHAPTER VIII.

THE TETRAGRAMMATON.

Such was the view which our Brethren of the last century took on this important subject; and in a short Essay on Freemasonry, prefixed to the first copy of the Laws and Regulations of the Royal Arch, which were agreed to in the year 1782 by the Constitutional Grand Lodge of England, and written, as I conceive, by Brother Dunckerley, some excellent observations on this Name occur, which merit preservation. "Speculative Masonry, or the Royal Arch, is subdivided into as many distinct branches as there are arts and sciences, and the parts as various as there are subjects for investigation; and we use certain signs, tokens, and words; but it must be observed that when we use that expression, and say THE WORD, it is not to be understood as a watchword only, after the manner of those annexed to the several degrees of the Craft, but also theologically as a term, thereby to convey to the mind some idea of that Great Being who is the sole author of our existence, and to carry along with it the most solemn veneration for his Sacred Name and

G 5

Word, as well as the most clear and perfect eluci-
dation of his power and attributes that the human
mind is capable of receiving. And that this is the
light in which the Name and Word hath always
been considered, from the remotest ages, not only
amongst us Christians and the Jews; but also in
the gentile or heathen world, may be clearly
understood from numberless writers; but to mention only two. Cicero tells us that they did not
dare to mention the names of their gods; and
Lucan says but to name the Name would shake
the earth. Amongst the Jews we all know with
what a just and awful veneration they look upon
it; which many of them carry so far as to believe
that but to pronounce the Word would be sufficient
to work wonders and remove mountains, and
therefore they never pronounce it.[1]

---

[1] There is an anecdote to the following effect told by Peter
de Natalibus. St. Sylvester, when disputing with certain Jews,
proved the faith of Christ by most evident reasons, and by the
sentence of the Judges, marvellously confuted them. And by
mutual consent, appealing to miracles, Zambri, a learned Jew,
who was also a magician, boasted that he knew the ineffable
Name of God, which no animal could hear and live. And a
bull was brought in, so ferocious as scarcely to be held by an
hundred men, and when Zambri whispered that Name in his ear,
roaring and with starting eyes, the bull fell down dead. And
the Jews thereupon exulting over Sylvester, the holy man
replied, that it was the name of a demon not a deity, that
destroyed life, while the tremendous Name of the true God, his
incarnate Son, would restore it even to the dead. Whereupon,
after invoking that Name, he bade the bull arise,—and he did
so, but with a changed nature, being now as tame and gentle as
before he was violent and savage.

"Josephus says that the Name [2] was never known till the time that God told it to Moses in the wilderness, and that he himself did not dare to mention it, for that it was forbidden to be used, except once in the year, by the High Priest alone, when he appeared before the Mercy Seat on the day of expiation.[3] He further adds that it was lost through the wickedness of man; and hence has arisen a difference of opinion; some supposing the Word itself lost; others, the import or meaning only; and many, the manner of its delivery, and from hence contend that Moses did not ask the Almighty for his name to carry to his brethren, but for the true delivery or pronunciation only. How far that might be the case, is to us uncertain; but it is certain that the true mode of delivery cannot now be proved from any written record; first, because it is capable of so many variations from the manner of annexing the Masoretic points, which points were not extant in the days of Moses; and secondly, because the language

[2] The Name here referred to is YEHOVAH ELOHIM, which is translated in the Scriptures, LORD GOD, and is the Name by which the Supreme Being was known from the creation of the world, and is used by the Jews at the present day.

[3] Hence the formula in our ceremonies, which is thus worded. "We have heard with our ears, and our fathers have declared unto us that in their time, and in times of old, it was not lawful for any one to mention the sacred and mysterious Name of the Most High, except the High Priest, and him but once a year, when he entered alone in the Sanctum Sanctorum, and stood before the Ark of the Covenant to make propitiation for the sins of the people."

now in use amongst the Jews is so corrupt and
altered from that in which he wrote, that none of
them, except some few of their learned, understand any thing of it; for which reason the Jews
call it שם המפורת Shem Hamphoreth, the unut-
terable Name. Hence is our learned brother,
Pythagoras, his τετραγραμματον or quaternion.

"Philo, the learned Jew, tells us not only that
the Word was lost, but also the time when, and
the reason why. But to make an end of these
unprofitable disputes among the learned, be it
remembered, that they all concur with Royal
Arch Masons in others much more essential;
first, that the Name or Word is expressive of
SELF-EXISTENCE AND ETERNITY; and secondly,
that it can be applicable only to that GREAT
BEING who WAS, who IS, and WILL BE.[4] It is also
generally allowed, that in its full sense and meaning, it must be incomprehensible by a human
capacity. Nevertheless we hope, so far as it hath
yet pleased the Omnipotent to reveal it, it is
reserved for the honour of this Society to show
forth to the world its Glory, Power, and Import,
in a much more perfect, clear, and ample manner,
than is now generally done."

[4] "This phraseology is purely Jewish," says Dr. Clark, "and
probably taken from the Tetragrammaton, יהוה', which is supposed to include in itself all time, past, present, and to come.
The time of prayer, as the Rabbins affirm, points out the holy
and blessed God; He who was, and is, and shall be. The
morning prayer points out Him who WAS before the foundation
of the world; the noonday prayer points out Him who IS; and
the evening prayer Him who IS TO COME."

These observations are very judicious, and served well to introduce the new degree, and recommend it to the notice of the Fraternity. It is much to be regretted, however, that Brother Dunckerley, whose influence in the Order was amply sufficient for the purpose, did not improve the degree from the materials which he derived from the *ancient* Masons, because he could not fail to perceive their incongruity, by at least a reconstruction of the Word which he has so learnedly described in the above cited passage; for whoever it might be that first arranged its members in their present form, certainly committed a capital error, and grievously mistook the principles on which the degree appears to have been founded.

It is doubted by some of the Rabbins whether the word Jehovah be the true Name of God, for they consider it to be irrecoverably lost by disuse;[5] and regard its pronunciation as one of the mysteries which will be revealed at the coming of the Messiah; and they attribute its loss to the illegality of applying the Masoretic points to such a Sacred Name, by which a knowledge of the proper vowels is forgotten. It is even said in the Gemara of Aboda Zara, that God permitted a celebrated Hebrew scholar to be burned by a

---

[5] When God, say the Rabbins, judgeth his creatures, his name is called ELOHIM; when he warreth against the wicked, it is called ISEBAOTH; but when he showeth mercy unto the world, he is called JEHOVAH.

Roman Emperor, because he had been heard to pronounce the Sacred name with points.

The author of the above tract, however, very properly alludes to the Tetragrammaton, or Word of four letters,[6] as forming the basis of the lost Word; which in the Jewish writings is spelled Jehovah or Jah. But in the forms which it now assumes it is either quadriliteral,[7] as יחזה, or biliteral, as יה, which is one of the titles of the Messiah, and plainly refers to the *advancing* of a R. A. Mason; for 3 + 5 + 7 are equal to 10 י + 5 ה = 15. This word, as numbered by the cabalists, is י, 10 + ה, 5 + ז, 6 + ה 5 = 26. The mystical cube and plumb-line, and the figures which compose it being added together give the number 8. Now the word IHΣOYΣ, corresponding with the above word יה, being numbered makes I, 10 + H, 8 + Σ, 200 + O, 70 + Y, 400 + Σ, 200 = 888, or THREE cubes. But the Royal Arch degree is founded on the number *three*, and therefore each member of the Word

---

[6] In the Samaritan, the Tetragrammaton, or word of four letters, is written thus ⳩⳦⳧ℿ, and the Jews even at the present day refuse either to write or utter it.

[7] "This name is written and pronounced by all nations with four letters. The Egyptians call him *Teut;* the Arabs, *Alla;* the Persians, *Sire;* the Magas, *Orsi;* the Mahometans, *Abdi;* the Greeks, *Teos;* the ancient Turks, *Esar;* and the Latins, *Deus;* to which John Lorrenzo Anani adds, the Germans call him *Gott;* the Surmatus, *Bouh* and *Istu;* the Tartars, *Itga;* the English, *Lord.* From which it is inferred that except by some divine inspiration, or from the knowledge they had of the Tetragrammaton of four letters, so many different nations could not agree. (Manasseh ben Israel, Concil. vol. ii. p. 194.)

ought to have been triliteral. Again, the cabalists used this form of the Word, which is an illustration of the same principle,

Sometimes expressed thus, triangularly,

```
            ה
          ה   ו
        ה   ו   ה
      ה   ו   ה   י
```

This designation of the Ineffable Name was a symbol of the creation; and the mysterious union of T. G A. O. T. U. with his creatures was in the letter ה He, which they considered to be the agent of Almighty power, and to enable the possessor of the Name to work miracles. It was also the symbol of the Trinity in Unity.

Amongst the Syrians, the Chaldeans, the Phœnicians, and others, the Ineffable Name of the Deity was Bel, Bal, Bul, Baal, or Belin. There are some doubts whether it was not biliteral; for we find אל El, בל Bel, and אב־אל Ab-El, signifying Pater Deus. The triliteral name was בעל Baal.

Again, the Egyptians and Hindoos reverenced On, or Om, *i.e.* Aun or Aum, as the name of their chief deity; who was also considered by the Canaanites as the Creator, or the prolific power, probably the solar orb; and the same name is compounded in the Philistine deity Dag-On, or in other words, the receptacle of On, which, perhaps, in their physical theology might refer to the ark of Noah. It is also found in the names of places in the same country, as Tzid-Aun (Sidon), Herm-On, Hebr-On, &c.; and the Chaldean Oannes was O-Aun-Nes. Amongst the Jews, during the Theocracy, the worship of Teraphim, whatever they might be, was connected with that of Aun. Thus the original of 1 Sam., xv. 23, is—" As the sin of divination is rebellion, so is *Aun* and Teraphim, stubbornness and iniquity." And the same thing occurred at a later period; thus Zechariah accuses them by saying, " Your Teraphim have announced Aun;" which in our translation is called " vanity," and was a solar oracle, which is nothing but vanity.[8] The fact appears to be, that they consulted the god Aun through the medium of the Teraphim, as Jehovah was consulted by Urim and Thummim,[9]

---

[8] Zech. x. 2.

[9] It was by means of the Urim and Thummim, that the High Priest obtained responses from God. " This utensil was certainly either connected or identical with the Breastplate, and on account of it that ornament itself was sometimes called the Breastplate of Judgment. Few readers would expect to derive this mystical badge from the ancient usages of Egypt, yet Sir J. G. Wilkinson says, that when a case was brought for trial there, it was customary for the arch Judge to put a golden chain around his neck, to which was suspended a small figure

or perhaps before the cherubic emblem, which is called by the Jews, " the very pith and marrow " of their mode of worship. Faber has taken a somewhat similar view of this subject, and concludes that, " by a plausible though wretched abuse, the Cherubim or Seraphim, or Teraphim, became the symbolic fatidical gods of paganism ; and as the principal hero-god of that system was thought to have migrated into the sun, and was thence astronomically worshipped as the solar deity, the Teraphim are, by the inspired writers, justly associated with the Egyptian On, who is the same as the Indo-Scythic Om of the Brahmins." [10]   It is remarkable that this word was also used by the early Christians to express the divine Being whom they worshipped, O ΩN, και ὁ ην, και ὁ ερχομενος, " God, which is, and was, and is to come." [11]   But it must be borne in mind that the heathen, while acknowledging their chief god to be the maker of the universe, did not understand it in the sense which we affix to it. They held that God built the world *out of existing materials;* while the Jews, as well as Christians, believe that he created it out of nothing.

---

of Teut, ornamented with precious stones. This appears to have been the origin of the Hebrew Thummim, a word implying Truth. And what makes it more remarkab'e is, that the chief priest of the Jews, who, before the election of a King, was also the Judge of the nation, was alone entitled to wear this honorary badge ; and the Thummim of the Hebrews, like the Egyptian figure, was studded with precious stones (Kitto).

[10] Eight Diss. vol. i. p. 391.

[11] Rev. i. 4.

The application of these materials to the purposes of Royal Arch Masonry would have been easy; and yet the usual combinations of them have failed to form a word in strict correspondence with the evident intention of the founders of the degree; for though it was termed the *fourth* degree, and included a reference to the Tetragrammaton, yet the TRIAD was considered to be its distinguishing element. The chief officers, the sojourners, the original Grand Lodges, the lights, the form of the jewels, and other particulars, are so many unanswerable proofs of it.[12] The frequent references to a trinity in unity, as well as the

[12] I subjoin a list of the Royal Arch Triads as they exist at the present time :—

Three Principals.
Three Grand Masters.
Three Sojourners.
Three Keystones.
Three Epochs.
Three Grand Lodges.
Three Lesser Lights.
Three Greater Lights.
Three Triangles.
Three Degrees.
The Triple Tau.
The Sacred Word.
A—B—L.
Father—Word—Spirit.
I A M.—Alpha—Omega.
Regal—Prophetical—Sacerdotal.
King—Prophet—Priest.
Historical—Symbolical—Mystical.
Holy—Sacred—Royal.
Patriarchal—Levitical—Christian.
Wisdom—Truth—Justice.

construction of the word itself, leave us no choice in the interpretation of the design which was intended to be conveyed in this sublime degree.

It was evidently a determination on the part of its founders to construct a link, by which Freemasonry might be unequivocally connected with Christianity; for the word, however it might be compounded, resolves itself into JEHOVAH, which, was the name of the divine Logos, or Christ being formed of יה, the *essence*, O ΩN, *He* who simply *is*, and הוה, *always existing*, which is the character assigned to Christ in the Apocalypse —"He who was, and is, and shall be—the

> Animal—Vegetable—Mineral.
> Water—Air—Fire.
> Bible—Square—Compasses.
> Vault—Cord—Shrine.
> Pickaxe—Crow—Shovel.
> Abraham—Isaac—Jacob.
> Moses—Aholiab—Bezaleel.
> S K I—H R T—H A B
> Solomon—Zerubbabel—Herod.
>
> { Judah—Issachar—Zebulon.
> { Lion—Ass—Ship.
> { Blue—Purple—Crimson.
>
> { Reuben—Simeon—Gad.
> { Man—Sword—Troop.
> { Red—Yellow—White.
>
> { Ephraim—Manasseh—Benjamin.
> { Ox—Vine—Wolf.
> { Green—Fleshcolour—Green.
>
> { Dan—Asher—Napthali.
> { Eagle—Vase—Hind.
> { Green—Purple—Blue.

Eternal." [13] This hypothesis is of sufficient importance to merit a free examination.

Before the fall of man we have plain indications of the appearance of JEHOVAH, or the WORD of God in paradise.[14] After our first parents had sinned, "they heard the VOICE of JEHOVAH walking in the garden." [15] Now, who was this "voice of Jehovah"? It could not be God the Father, because St. John positively affirms that "no man hath seen GOD at any time." [16] And adds, that "he declares himself by means of his only begotten Son." It must therefore have been Christ, who is called elsewhere, "the Angel of the Covenant," "the Branch," "Jehovah our Righteousness," &c., that thus conferred with our erring progenitors. This is confirmed by the terms of the prophecy of Balaam, who calls his victorious Star, who is to smite and annihilate the worshippers of On and Om, Aun, and Baal Peor, by this very title of the "Voice of Jehovah." [17] This appears to have been the opinion of the early Christians, for Theophilus Antiochenus [18] says expressly, "the Word, or voice of God, came into paradise and talked with Adam."

This is the sense in which the passage is explained by the Targumists; for they agree to render it, "they heard the WORD of the Lord God walking," &c.; the Jerusalem Targum paraphrases the beginning of Gen. iii. 9, by "the

---

[13] Rev. xi. 17.
[15] Gen. iii. 8.
[17] Numb. xxiv. 17.
[14] Gen. ii. 16—18.
[16] John i. 18.
[18] Ad Autol. l. 2.

WORD of the Lord called unto Adam." The word, therefore, that called was the word or voice that walked." [19] Indeed, the old Chaldee paraphrase, the Jerusalem Targum, and the most learned rabbinical commentators, interpret Jehovah who communed with Adam to be the Memra or Messias. And Jonathan and Onkelos add, that "he judged the old world by his Word;" that he "made a covenant with Abraham by his Word;" and that "he would redeem mankind by his Word." [20]

In like manner, Christians of all ages and times have held the opinion, that Jehovah who appeared to man in the time of the patriarchs was Christ. Thus, for example, that which the angel spake to Hagar [21] is said to be spoken by Jehovah,[22] and the same angel said, "I am the God (Jehovah or El Shaddai) of Bethel." [23] This angel, who is styled in other places the Angel of the Covenant,[24] the Angel of God's presence,[25] and the Name of God,[26] was no other than our Lord Jesus Christ, according to the unanimous opinion of all antiquity.

If further proofs of this invaluable truth be wanting, they are at hand. The Almighty says,

---

[19] See Maimon. Mor. Nevich. p. i. c. 24 ; Tzet. Hammor. s. Beresh. apud Owen. Exerc. x. in Heb. vi. 1 ; Faber, Eight Diss. i. 28.

[20] Jerusalem Targum on Gen. xlix. 18.

[21] Gen. xvi. 7—11. [22] Gen. xvi. 13.

[23] Gen. xxxi. 13. [24] Mal. iii. 1.

[25] Isai. lxiii. 9. [26] Exod. xxiii. 21.

by the prophet Isaiah,[27] "I am Jehovah, and there
is none else ; there is no God besides me." But
St. John says, " the Word was God ; "[28] and St.
Paul affirms, " Christ came, who is God over all ;
God blessed for ever."[29]   Therefore Christ is
Jehovah or God.   The glorious Name which was
given to Moses at the burning bush,[30] was assumed
by Christ himself, when he said,[31] " Before Abraham was, I AM," not *I was*, but I AM.[32]   This
name, אהיה, is therefore esteemed by the modern
Jews inferior to the Tetragrammaton, because,
they say, though it demonstrates the divine
essence, yet it forms only a part of that sacred
name ; for numerically it is only twenty-one,
while the Tetragrammaton is twenty-six.

The most ancient Jewish writers, instead of
Jehovah use the name *Memra*, by which they
intend to signify the Son of God.[33] Now,

---

[27] Isai. xlv. 5.   [28] John i. 1.

[29] Rom. i. 8.   [30] Exod. iii. 14.

[31] John viii. 58.

[32] There was an inscription placed above the door of the
Temple of Apollo at Delphi, consisting of a simple monosyllable,
E I, THOU ART, which was the second person of the Greek
substantive verb ειμι, I AM. On this word Plutarch wrote a large
treatise, which he concluded thus :—" This word corresponds
to certain others on the same Temple, viz., ΓΝΩΘΙ ΣΕΑΥΤΟΝ,
KNOW THYSELF ; as if, under the name E I, THOU ART, the
deity designed to excite men to venerate Him as eternally
existing, and to put them in mind of the frailty and mortality
of their own nature."

[33] One would think from the following passage that Dr. Adam
Clarke was a Royal Arch Mason. He says in his annotation on
Ezek. xxxiv. 29.—" He is elsewhere called a BRANCH and a

as some of these learned men lived before and about the time of Christ, their opinions on this point may be received as positive evidence of the fact. In the passages of their sacred writings, where the name of Jehovah occurs, they substitute MEMRA JEHOVAH, or the Word of God, to whom they ascribe the creation of the world, as we do to Christ; and all the divine manifestations which we find there, they say were effected by Memra.

In addition to this evidence, which is exceedingly valuable, we may also remark that in our authorized translation of the Scriptures the Septuagint version has been followed in rendering the word Jehovah by $K\nu\rho\iota o\varsigma$, or Lord; and whenever the word LORD appears in the English Bible, it stands for Jehovah in the original; to which name the Jews associate much superstition and mystery. Many of the ancient fathers assert, that in their copies of the Bible the Name was written in Samaritan characters, that it might not be polluted by the heathen.

If to the above reasoning we subjoin the testimony of early Christian writers on this point, it will complete the chain of evidence, that the name

ROD, being *the person of Name—*JESUS; *the Saviour,* CHRIST; *the Anointer* long spoken of before he was manifested in the flesh, and for ever afterwards the daily theme in the Church militant; no other Name being given amongst men by which we can be saved; he who has a Name above every Name, and at whose Name every knee shall bow; through whose Name, by faith in his Name, the diseased are healed; and in whose Name all our prayers and supplications must be presented to God to make them acceptable. *This is the Person of* NAME."

of Jehovah, and the Word spoken of by St. John, and inserted in the Tracing-board of the English Royal Arch are one and the same person. Justin Martyr[34] says—"Our Christ conversed with Moses out of the bush in the appearance of fire." And again[35]—"It was the Son of God who spoke to Moses," saying, I AM THAT I AM. Thus shalt thou say unto the Children of Israel, I AM hath sent me unto you.[36] Irenæus affirms,[37] that "it was the Word of God who, in a divine and glorious manner, conversed with the patriarchs." Tertullian is equally decisive on the subject, when he tells his adversary that it was Christ who conversed upon earth from the beginning; and that it was He who appeared on all occasions to the patriarchs and the prophets."[38] Athanasius, Hilary, Basil, and Cyril of Jerusalem, speak to the same effect; and our Bishop Bull affirms that it was the unanimous opinion of all primitive antiquity.

[34] Apol. 1.   [35] Apol. 2.

[36] "These words have been variously understood. The Vulgate translates *Ego sum qui sum, I am who am.* The Septuagint, Εγω ειμι οδον, *I am he who exists.* The Syriac, the Persic, and the Chaldee preserve the original words without any gloss. The Arabic paraphrases them, *The Eternal, who passes not away.* The Targum of Jonathan, and the Jerusalem Targum paraphrase the words thus—*He who spake and the world was; who spake and all things existed.*" (Clarke on Exod. iii. 14.)

[37] L. iii. c. 11.   [38] Adv. Marc. l. ii. 4, 27.

CHAPTER IX.

THE INSIGNIA.

A FURTHER proof of the Christian reference of the Royal Arch degree is found, not only in certain passages of the lectures which represent "the way, the truth, and the life," as characteristic of the Redeemer, and a direct mention of "the second person in the glorious Trinity," but also in its characteristic symbol or mark; for the TRIPLE TAU [1] was unknown before the dispensation of Christ was promulgated, and the main hinge, on which all its illustrations were suspended, was the advent of Shiloh when the sceptre had departed from Judah. Now a sceptre, being figuratively put for government, because it is an ensign of royalty, it referred *literally* to the just and righteous government of King Solomon, but

---

[1] This figure forms two right angles on each of the exterior lines, and another at the centre by their union, for the three angles of each triangle are equal to two right angles. This being triplified illustrates the jewel worn by the Companions of the Royal Arch, which by its intersection, forms a given number of angles. These may be taken in five several combinations, and being reduced, their amount in right angles will be found equal to the five Platonic bodies, which represent the four elements, and the sphere of the universe.

mystically to the government of Christ, which is more just and righteous, over the faithful people of God, and is therefore emphatically called "a sceptre of righteousness." [2]

The Jews, however, affect to believe that the word *shebet* in the Hebrew text, which we interpret a sceptre, signifies a rod, which is an instrument of chastisement; and therefore they contend that it means, that their dispersion amongst strange nations shall not cease till their Messiah shall come to deliver them from it. Christ began his public ministry at a solemn jubilee; and therefore he said—"The Lord hath anointed me (as the Christ) to preach the gospel to the poor, he hath sent me (as Shiloh, or the Apostle) to heal the broken hearted, to proclaim deliverance to the captives, and restoration of sight to the blind, to set at liberty the bruised, and to preach the acceptable year of the Lord." [3] Mr. Taylor, after proving satisfactorily that the Shiloh here mentioned could be no other than Christ, adds—"Our Lord was the only branch of David's family entitled to rule, [4] and if the royalty had continued in that family, he would have sat upon the throne of Israel; and he dying without issue, the ruling branch of that family became extinct; so that,

---

[2] Heb. i. 8.   [3] Luke iv. 18.

  [4] From Jesse's root behold a BRANCH arise,
     Whose sacred flower with fragrance fills the skies;
     Th' ethereal Spirit o'er its leaves shall move,
     And on its top descends the mystic dove.
                         Pope's " Messiah."

after his death, there was no longer any possibility of the continuance of the kingly office in the direct and proper line of David. The person who should have held the sceptre was dead ; the direct descent of the family expired with him, the sceptre was *bonâ-fide* departed ; since, first it was actually swayed by a stranger or strangers (Herod and the Romans) ; and, secondly, no one who could possibly claim it, though he might have been of a collateral branch of David's house, could have been the direct legal claimant by birthright; for that person was crucified ! ; Such is the language Providence put into the mouth of Pilate—'SHALL I CRUCIFY YOUR KING?' 'Yes,' say the Jews, 'we reject the lineal descendant of David, and prefer Cæsar.' Rome triumphs ; David expires in the person of his son; and with him expires all direct claim of right to the sceptre. The sceptre is departed from David, and if from David—from Judah—JESUS OF NAZARETH, THE KING OF THE JEWS ! ''[5]

In the Royal Arch degree the name of God is depicted in the medal of the Order, as in the centre of our Floor-cloth, and also in the jewel of the Grand Superintendent, by a double interlacing triangle, thus ✡, inscribed within a dark circle, representing unlimited space beyond the reach of light, and the top representing the "light shining in darkness, and the darkness comprehending it not," as a continuation of the divine

---

[5] Taylor's Calmet in loc.

sentence at the summit of the Floor-cloth.[6] This
had been used as a Christian symbol, to denote
the two natures of Jehovah, the God-man, for
centuries before the Royal Arch degree was ever
thought of. In this form ☆, or the above, it was
called the pentangle, or seal of Solomon, and the
shield of David, and was employed all over Asia
as a preservative against witchcraft, in which
superstition the Jews are said to have participated;[7]
for they used written charms inclosed in the
above hexagonal or pentangular figure, and disposed cabalistically, which were worn about their
necks. It constituted the Pythagorean pentalpha,
and was the symbol of health. Thus Pitrius says,

⁶ John i. 5.

⁷ A learned and much esteemed brother Mason writes to me
thus :—"There appears to have been a great veneration for the
pentalpha ☆ as a charm against any evil, and even to have
been in use amongst the ancient Jews as a symbol betokening
safety, and as representing ΥΓΙΕΙΑ, *Health;* no doubt its allusion
to the Tree of Life, whose leaves are for the healing of the
nations ; or to the Star in the East, which arose in the midst of
so much moral darkness in the Jewish Church ; when all was
dark save one glimmering Star in the East, referring to the Sun
of Righteousness, which shall arise with healing in his wings ;—
that bright and Morning Star, whose rising bringeth peace and
salvation to the faithful and obedient of the human race."

"Pentagonum, salutis symbolum fuisse; autem illi hujusmodi ostendisse, triangulum triplicem invicem insertum ex lineis quinque constantem; in quibus ΥΓΙΕΙΑ scriptum erat. Sic enim salus sanitasve Græce apellatur."

Christians used it to represent the five wounds of Christ, thus; and hence it was formerly referred,

in the old lectures of Masonry, to the birth, life, death, resurrection, and ascension of the Saviour of mankind. And the formula which was used, even so recently as the early part of my Masonic life, is worth preserving.

"What do we learn by his birth? He being the day-star of mercy, hath risen to conduct our feet in the paths of peace and holiness.

"What by his life? All the moral and social virtues, he being the way, the truth, and the life.

"What by his death? That our debt is paid, the law satisfied, and our redemption completed.

"What by his resurrection? A victory over death and the grave, wherein resteth our justification.

"What by his ascension? That he is gone before to prepare a place for his faithful people, that where he is, there may they be also."

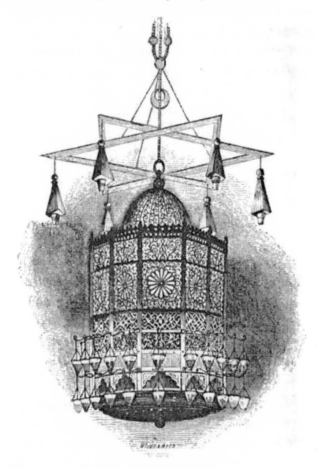

The above symbol is very common in Asia, even at the present day. Mr. Drummond Hay, speaking of the ornaments in the harem of a Moor, mentions "a brass frame composed of two intersecting triangles, as a chandelier." These kind of lamps or lanterns are very common ; and in the palace of a monarch they are often of great magnificence. I subjoin an engraving of one of these lanterns, with the pentangle of Solomon attached.[8]

The next great and distinguishing symbol of the Royal Arch degree is the tau cross triplified, ☖. It is inscribed equally on the flap of the apron and on the Jewel of the G. Standard bearer, in a triangle, and also at the foot of theMedal in a circle. And as the former was the seal of Solomon, and considered capable of warding off earthly dangers, so is this the seal of Christ, and competent to guard the recipient from such dangers as are spiritual.[9] This latter seal is baptism, accompanied by the crucial sign. Thus Valesius and others expound it and term it " the seal of our Lord," because in the very nature of it there is contained a covenant made between God and man, of which the sign or symbol of the cross is

----

[8] In the " Landmarks of Masonry," this pentangular symbol is fully illustrated ; and I refer the curious reader to vol. ii. pp. 355 and 659, for further information ; and some remarks may also be found in the " Theocratic Philosophy," p. 169.

[9] The Seal of Solomon was believed by the Arabians to possess incredible power over the evil genii. By virtue of the Name which was engraven in cipher on this Seal, Solomon subjected them to his dominion. And it is also believed that by its efficacy the dead may be raised. Lane tells us, that there are other names of the Deity which have a peculiar efficacy when uttered or written. " Of such names and invocations, together with words unintelligible to those who are ignorant of the science of divine magic, passages from the Koran, mysterious combinations of numbers, and peculiar diagrams and figures, are chiefly composed written charms employed for good purposes only."

the seal. Hence Thecla said to St. Paul—" Give me the seal of Christ, and no temptation shall have power over me." And the Shepherd Hermas, speaking of some who had died after baptism, says,—" They were sealed with the seal of the Son of God, and are entered into the kingdom of God. For before a person receives the sign of the Son of God, he is consigned over to death; but when he receives that seal, he is freed from death and consigned over to life." And hence the cross was the symbol of life; and when triplified, it was an emblem of life eternal.

This remarkable figure, at its first construction, was an emblem used by the eastern Christians as a monogram of the sacred name of Christ. The original form appears to have been this ☧, a combination of the Greek XP (Chr),[10] the two first letters in ΧΡΙΣΤΟΣ; and it was placed, as a talisman of protection on the summit of the ensign staff by Constantine; thus occupying the same honourable position as the Egyptian ibis, the

---

[10] " The bas-reliefs of the ancient *ambones* of the cathedral of Rouen, now incrusted into the wall behind the choir, are curious as exhibiting, in distinct rows, the fish, the dove, the lamb, the stag, the peacock, &c., the whole sacred menagerie, as Mr. Hope calls it, of symbolism. These tombs throw an interesting light on the origin of three tufts or rays of glory, emblematical of the Trinity, which surround our Saviour's head in the productions of early Italian painting, and even in the early works of Raphael, Titian, and their contemporaries. I have little doubt of their being a corruption of the well-known monogram of our Saviour's name, formed by the Greek letters X and P." (Lord Lindsay's Christian Art, vol. i. p. 03.)

Athenian owl, or the Roman eagle. It soon became a universal Christian symbol, although the form of its construction underwent many variations, as may be seen in that curious work of Aringhius, called "Roma Subterranea;" amongst which is found the triple tau of our Royal Arch degree, and the motto was IN HOC SIGNO VINCES! It was subsequently transferred to the official seals of several Roman pontiffs; from whence it passed into general use in all Christian countries; and formed part of an inscription on an old bell formerly in Great Grimsby Church, of which I subjoin a correct copy.

𝕮𝖆𝖔𝖎𝖚𝖚 𝖎𝖆𝖊

𝖕𝖑𝖆𝖈𝖊𝖆𝖙 𝖙𝖚𝖎 𝖈𝖊𝖄

𝖈𝖔𝖚𝖚𝖘 𝕩𝖎𝖗

The above monogram merged into the triple tau during the life-time of Constantine, and appears not only on his coins, but on those of his successors; and certain contractions afterwards sprang into use, which were as highly reverenced as the original symbol. First we find the two first letters in the Greek name of Jesus, IHΣOΥΣ, used as a monogram, or mysterious sign, to represent the name of Jehovah or Christ, which were sometimes so disposed as to form the triple tau, the I being placed upon the H in the form of a cross, thus ⊞; and subsequently, when the third letter of the above name Σ or C, was added, the symbol assumed this form I⊞C, for which the Western Church substituted the Roman letters

IħS, which are still profusely used by the Roman Catholics; and many Protestant pulpits are inscribed with the sacred I⊞S.[11]

The above are the initial letters of the Greek inscription placed by Pilate on the cross of our blessed Saviour, of which I subjoin a fac-simile, taken by Dr. Adam Clarke from a copy of the *Codex Bezæ*, which was first delineated in the fourth century, and resembles the autographs of the earliest ages of Christianity.

IHCOYC O NAZ⍵ƑEOC·
O BΛCIΛEYC ΥⲰN
IOYΔΛiⲰN´

---

[11] In a letter which I received some years ago; from Brother Willoughby, of Birkenhead, he says—"I was struck with an observation which fell from an old Scottish Mason, who was exalted on our last Chapter day. After the ceremony he was looking round the room, in order to take a calmer view of the arrangements, and seeing the ⊞ upon the plinth of the altar,

It is well known that the Greek Σ was anciently constructed like the Roman C, and was so used for several centuries; and therefore the IHC of the Eastern Church was improperly changed by its rival of the West to the Roman IHS.

Occasionally we find an abbreviation of both the names of Christ used as a monogram; thus IC XC, because these letters were supposed to represent the position of Christ's right hand when elevated in benediction; as M. Didron explains it, " L'index s'alonge comme un I; le grand doigt se courbe comme un C, ancien *sigma* des Grecs, le pouce et l'annulaire se croisent pour faire un X, et le petit doigt s'arrondit pour figurer un C. Tout cela IC-XC, monogramme Grec de Jesus Christ ('IησοῦC XριστοC)."[12] It was sometimes expressed I ⳨ C XC, and sometimes XPC. And it does not vitiate the argument to consider that this monogram I⳨S was the mysterious badge of the Jesuits, and worn upon the sleeve of their garments;[13] as if, to use the language of Henry

he asked me, 'What are you doing with that figure here?' 'Why do you ask?' said I. 'Because it is what we call the Holy Jesus,' was his reply. He is a builder in an extensive way, and said that he had often met with it in old churches, and that it was always called 'The Holy Jesus,' or Jesus the Saviour of Mankind, IHS."

[12] Icon. de Dieu, p. 212.

[13] For the prophet Ezekiel was divinely directed to "set a mark on the foreheads of the men that cry against the abomina- tions of the people." This custom was used by almost all nations. The worshippers of particular idols usually bore the mark of their favourite deity on their foreheads. These sectarian marks are still used in the East Indies.

Burton, "with the name of Jesvs, inchanter-like, they would coniure downe the spirit of truthe, and coniure vp the spirit of pontifician errour and sedition againe in this our churche."[14] It rather confirms our view of the subject, by showing that this tau or cross was publicly used and sanctioned for ages by the highest authorities of the Christian church.

Another form which this ever-varying monogram assumed was the *vesica piscis*,[15] an ancient Platonic symbol, but identified with Christ (and in a fresco painting of the Last Judgment, in the chapel of the Arena at Padua, by Giotti, the Saviour is represented as seated within the vesica piscis[16]), by the substitution of the Greek word

---

[14] Triall of Private Devotions, A.D. 1625.

[15] The vesica piscis contains the well-known geometrical outline of a Fish, and received its name from the Greek word Ιχθυος, which is an acrostic of the name of the Redeemer of mankind; Ιησοῦς Χριστος Θεοῦ Υιὸς Ο Σωτήρ, whence it became an emblem of Christ; although it had been used geometrically long before his personal advent into the world. It appertained to the Platonic system, and constituted the' sign of recognition amongst the Epopts of the mysteries, by the open hands united with the ends of the fingers, and wrists touching each other. Vesica piscis often occurs in the Egyptian temples, and particularly about the throne of Osiris, in reference to the divine Triads, and geometrically represents the birth of Light, Horus, or the Sun, from the wedding of Osiris and Isis.— From an unpublished MS. on the Discrepancies of Masonry, ut supra, where the subject is scientfically handled, and illustrated by a series of Masonic and geometrical diagrams.

[16] "Amongst the Mosaics in the nave of St. Maria Maggiore at Rome, we find a design of the Israelites stoning Moses and Aaron in their flight to the tabernacle, on the morning after the

for a fish, IXΘΥΣ, the letters of which formed the initials of the name and character of the Redeemer. Ιησοῦς Χριστος Θεοῦ Υιος Σωτὴρ, *Jesus Christ, the Son of God, our Saviour.* We frequently find, not only in Freemasonry but elsewhere, the addition of the Greek letters A and Ω subjoined to all and each of the above-mentioned monograms, to denote the eternity of Christ as Jehovah. Thus Ducange—

> Circulus hic summi comprendit nomina regis,
> Quem sine principio et sine fine vides.
> Principium cum fine simul tibi donat A cum Ω ;
> X et P Christi nomina sancta tenent.[17]

punishment of Korah, Dathan, and Abiram, a hand from heaven surrounds them with a *vesica piscis,* from which the stones, arrested, fall innocuously to the ground ; while a third figure (like the fourth in the fiery furnace of the three children) appears beside them, within the vesica piscis, intended doubtless for our Saviour." (Lord Lindsay, ut supra, p. 101.)

[17] Gloss. v. 10, apud Io. Anton. Castill. de antiquitate Basil.

CHAPTER X.

THE SYMBOLS.

WE will now examine how far this doctrine is applicable to Royal Arch Masonry. We are taught by our Fiducial Sign that if we prostrate ourselves with our faces to the earth, it is to implore the mercy of Jehovah our Creator and Judge (or in other words T.G.A.O.T.U., for as Christians we believe Him to be our Creator, and look for no other judge), relying with humble confidence on his most gracious promises, by which alone we hope to pass through the Ark of our Redemption into the mansion of eternal bliss and glory, the presence of Him who is the great I AM, the Alpha and Omega, the beginning and the ending, the first and the last. It appears from evidence which is incontrovertible, that this great and holy Being was known under the same NAME, or one which very nearly resembled it, in almost every nation under the canopy of heaven, however they might have departed from the true faith and manner of worship. By one he was called Ivah, or Evah; by another, Javoh; by others, Jevah, Jove, Jupiter, &c. Macrobius, in his Saturnalia (1. i. 18), says, that it was an admitted axiom amongst the heathen, that the triliteral JAH, or rather IAΩ, was the sacred name of the Supreme God. And the Clarian oracle, which was of unknown antiquity, being asked which of the deities was named IAΩ, answered in these memorable words:—

"The initiated are bound to conceal the mysterious secrets. Learn thou, that IAΩ is the Great God Supreme, who ruleth over all."

Now it so happens, that in the gems of the earliest Christians we find these very letters, IAΩ, which are an abbreviation of JEHOVAH, used as a monogram to express the name of the Saviour of mankind, who was thus represented as existing before time was, and shall exist when time shall be no more. It was first adopted by the Eastern church, and signified Ιησους, Αλφα Ωμεγα, Jesus, Alpha Omega, or in other words, Jesus, the first and the last.[1] And this is consonant with the decision of Ducange, who says that the letters A and Ω "designantes Christi divinitatem et humanitatem," like the intersecting triangles of the English Royal Arch.

But this appropriation of A and Ω to Jesus Christ does not rest on the opinions of men, but it is frequently and plainly proclaimed in the Word of God. Jehovah applies it to himself in these remarkable words—"Thus saith Jehovah, the King of Israel, his Redeemer, the Lord of

---

[1] Rev. xxii. 18.

Hosts, *I am the first, and I am the last,* and besides me there is no other God."[2] But Jesus Christ claims these titles—" Behold I come quickly, to give to every man according as his work shall be. I am Alpha and Omega, the beginning and the end, *the first and the last.*"[3] And again, in another place—" I am A and Ω the beginning and the ending, which is, and was, and is to come, the Almighty."[4] And he glories in the title, which his beloved disciple attributes to him saying—"These things saith the First and the Last, that was dead and is alive."[5] On this account it was that he commenced his Gospel with that memorable passage which occupies such a prominent situation on the old Royal Arch Tracing-boards—" In the beginning was the WORD," that is, A and Ω; and more significantly expressed in the central symbol of the sacred name. But his eternity is more plainly avouched by St. Paul. The royal prophet David had said—"They all shall wax old, as doth a garment, and as a vesture shalt thou change them and they shall be changed; but THOU art the same, and Thy years shall not fail."[6] These very words are applied by the apostle to Jesus Christ;[7] and again,[8] he says—" Jesus Christ is the same yesterday, to-day, and for ever;" which was an appropriation of the words of Jehovah by the prophet —"I am Jehovah, I change not."[9]

---

[2] Isaiah xliv. 6.   [3] Rev. xxii. 12, 13.   [4] Rev. i. 8.
[5] Rev. ii. 8.   [6] Psalm cii. 27.   [7] Heb. xi. 11, 12.
[8] Heb. xiii. 8.   [9] Mal. iii. 6.

The Royal Arch work, to have been perfectly in keeping with the degree, and with the general construction of Masonry, should have been a triad not only of syllables but also of letters. Our transatlantic Brethren have seen this in its true light; but they have corrected the error unlearnedly. It ought to have been, if the principle of its construction be allowed, to be orthodox.

Syriac	Chaldee	Hindoo

And to have made it intelligible to a mere English scholar, which description will apply to a great majority of Royal Arch Masons, it should be translated to them thus—

English	English	English

I cannot be more explicit for obvious reasons; but every Companion of the Order will be at no loss to understand my meaning.

Having thus, at some length, explained the tendency and various significations of that magnificent and sublime symbol which occupies the centre of the Floor-cloth, as it was understood by our Brethren of the last century—the Deity surrounded by infinite universal space; his eternity being declared by the awful EN APXH HN O ΛΟΓΟΣ, which forms the crowning glory of the design—"The light shining in darkness, and the darkness comprehending it not;" I proceed to an examination of the subordinate figures, which constitute so many symbols, or types, illustrative of the doctrine which has already been

I

enunciated, the chief of which had been abstracte from the third degree.

The diagrams underneath the centre arch consist of two single triads of circles, and a figure composed of three sides of a square, combining seven circles, and representing the TETRAGRAMMATON in the ancient Alphabet, called by the name of SOL. The vertical triad refers either to the three original Grand Lodges on mounts Sinai and Horeb, each governed by as many Grand Masters; or to the three Principals of the Chapter, symbolized by the three key-stones, to show that as a knowledge of certain mysterious secrets was attained by drawing them forth, so by passing through these offices [10] a knowledge of the arcana of Royal Arch Masonry may be successfully accomplished. Now these three Principals are described in the original rules of the degree (A.D. 1782) thus:—"The three Principals in Chapter assembled are to be considered conjunctly, as THE MASTER, and each severally as A MASTER." [11] Hence in their aggregate capacity

---

[10] Thus it is enacted that "no companion shall be installed in the second chair who has not served in the third chair, nor in the first unless he has served in the second chair of a regularly constituted chapter, for the full period from one annual election to another."

[11] Which is thus explained in the general regulations. "According to ancient custom, a complete chapter of this order of Freemasonry consists of three principals, who, when in Chapter assembled, are to be considered conjointly as the master, and severally as a master, two scribes, three sojourners, and others, making up the number of 72 as a Council; and no regular Chapter can consist of more; but any number may be

they represent ONE PERSON only, in whom is
united the different attributes of king, priest, and
prophet. For as there is a trinity of persons in
the Godhead,[12] so there was a trinity of offices
combined in the second person when incarnate,
which is clearly represented in the diagram.
Now it will be observed that these Principals
are three only in name, not in office. They are
not 1 Z, 2 H, 3 J, but

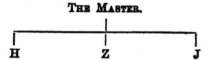

They are therefore typical of Jehovah-Christ,
in whom these offices are permanently united in
their utmost perfection, and in him alone. This
arrangement is one of the great beauties of the
degree.

It is possible that the angular triad might bear
a further reference to the three great lights, which
were at that period interpreted to symbolize " the
light of the gospel, and the sublime mystery of

exalted and received as companions, though they are not to
hold the staff of office, or to be considered as councillors when
more than that number are present." Hence it is further
directed that "each of the Grand Principals before being
inducted into his office shall be installed a principal Z."

[12] The Continental Masons of the last century ascribed three-
symbolic centres to the Deity. 1. The TRINITY breathing on
the abyss at the creation. 2. WISDOM, or the Eternal Word
passing, at the same period, through the different stages of
delight, desire, and strife, into fire or light; and this was denominated the great mystery. 3. The Logos, Jehovah, Word,
or T. G. A. O. T. U.

the trinity." The linear triad bore an allusion to the sojourners, who represented the three stones on which prayers and thanksgivings were offered on the discovery of the lost WORD; thereby affording an example, that it is our duty in every important undertaking, to offer up our prayers and thanksgivings to the God of our salvation. While the quadrangular diagram reminds us of the seven pair of pillars which supported King Solomon's private avenue, the seven steps in advancing, and the seven seals; for in those days the OB was sealed seven times.

The figures, however, being read from right to left, may have a reference to the three degrees of Craft Masonry, the three divisions of Operative, and the seven divisions of Speculative Masonry; the latter of which, in those times, was identified with the Royal Arch degree, and referred to the seven liberal sciences; and both were thus explained in the lectures of the day:—

"Freemasonry is to be considered as divided into two parts, the operative and the speculative; and these are again subdivided, the operative (that is Craft Masonry) into three distinct branches, the manual, the instrumental, and the scientific. The manual consists of such parts of business as are performed by hand-labour alone, or by the help of some simple instruments, the uses whereof are not to be learnt by any problems or rules of art, but by labour and practice only; and this is more peculiarly applicable to our Brethren of the first degree, called Entered Apprentices.

" The instrumental consists in the use and application of various tools and implements, such as the common gage, the square, the plumb-line, the level, and others that may be called mathematical, invented to find the size or magnitude of the several parts or materials whereof our buildings are composed, to prove when they are wrought into due form and proportion, and when so wrought, to fix them in their proper places and positions; and likewise to take the dimensions of all bodies, whether plain or solid, and to adjust and settle the proportions of space and extent. To this part also belongs the use of various other instruments or machines, such as the lever, the wheel and axle, the wedge, the screw, the pulley, &c., which may be called mechanic, being used to forward and expedite our business, to alleviate our toils, and enable us to perform that by a single hand, which could not be done without many, and in some cases not at all; and those more properly belong to our Brethren of the second degree, styled Fellowcrafts.

" The scientific consists in the knowledge of several of the arts and sciences, so far as to enable us to discern the reason for the operations of those before-mentioned instruments, tools, and machines, and to calculate the force and momentum of the different mechanical powers; and also to clear up and arrange our ideas in such a manner, as to be able to delineate them so clearly on our Tracing-board, that, by the help of a proper scale, our Brethren of the second degree may take them

off and complete our design, and, if intended for
that purpose, erect a structure, which, when
finished, shall contain the greatest possible degree
of strength, elegance, and convenience, that the
quantity of materials and space allowed will admit
of; and this is the part of, or applicable to, our
Brethren of the highest degree of the Craft of
Master Masons.

"To each of these degrees belong certain signs,
tokens, and watchwords, well known amongst the
Brethren, and also a variety of instructive maxims
and apothegms, the former intended to detect
impostors, and exclude the unworthy from their
Lodges; and the latter to strengthen the memory,
to correct the judgment, and habituate the mind
by a due course of reasoning, to trace up causes
from effects, and thereby explode the dogmata of
every false hypothesis; and thus we are handed
on from infancy to childhood, from childhood to
youth, from youth to manhood; and by the in-
structions received in passing through the several
probationary degrees of the Craft, are prepared
for our own most sublime one, namely, speculative
Masonry, or the Royal Arch, intended for the
cultivation of every art and science that the human
mind, in this sublunary state, is capable of; and
particularly the seven liberal sciences, which are
so many branches of that universal science called
Freemasonry;" which may account for the seven
circles in the quadrangular figure before us.

The remaining emblems mostly belong to the
third degree, although, for a brief period, they

were incorporated into the Royal Arch, as apposite illustrations of the lucid emblem in the centre of the Tracing-board. They were appendages equally to the tabernacle of Moses and the temple of Solomon; but were not all restored after it had been rebuilt by Zerubabel. We have here the golden candlestick, the table of shewbread, the censer or altar of incense, the pot of manna, and Aaron's rod. These were explained in the following manner:—

The candlestick was manufactured by Bezaleel and Aholiab of beaten gold. It had an upright shaft, which stood on a broad foundation, that its support might be firm and immoveable, without danger of being overthrown during the process of trimming and cleaning its lamps, which were seven in number (although nine are represented in the figure), one in the centre, and three on each side, on so many branches, that were not equal in length, the outer branches being elongated, that the lights might be all of the same height. The body of the shaft had four bowls, and as many knops and flowers, from which the branches sprang; each branch containing the same number of bowls, knops, and flowers. Some think that the seven branches symbolized the seven planets, the seven days of the week, and the seven ages of man; but, in truth, the Christian church is the candlestick, and the light is Christ.[13] The seven lamps are emblems of the

[13] Rev. i. 20.

gifts of the Spirit; the knops and flowers, the graces and ornaments of a Christian life. As the candlestick gave light to the tabernacle, so we must remain in darkness unless Christ shall enlighten his church.[14] Simeon, therefore, pronounced it to be "a light to lighten the Gentiles, and the glory [15] of Israel.[16]

On the opposite side of the sacred symbol we find the table of shewbread. Moses was commanded to construct this table of shittim wood, because it was intended to be durable, and to last as long as the Jewish dispensation should continue. This wood was the *acacia*, which, according to Kitto,[17] was exclusively employed in the construction of the tabernacle. It is well agreed by writers on the natural history of the

[14] The Lights in our present Chapters are placed singly, and in number six,—three greater and three lesser. The latter allude to the patriarchal, Mosaical, and Christian dispensations, while the three greater represent the SACRED NAME itself, expressive of his creative, preserving, and destroying power. These Lights are placed in the form of an equilateral triangle, each of the lesser intersecting the line formed by the two greater; thus geometrically dividing the greater triangle into three lesser triangles, at its extremities, and by their union form a fourth triangle in the centre, all of them being equal and equilateral, emblematical of the three degrees in Masonry, the E. A. P., the F. C., and the M. M., including the holy Royal Arch.

[15] *Nimbus*, referring to the glory which played round the head of Moses when he came down from the mount, and thus preserving a common phraseology, characteristic of the rays of light within the interlacing triangles of our Tracing-board, and overshadowing the altar of incense.

[16] Luke ii. 32.

[17] Palestine, ccli.

Bible, that the shittim wood was afforded by a
species of acacia; but the particular species has
been less determinately mentioned. But now
that the labours of the French commission, and
of different recent travellers, have made us acquainted with the botany of Arabia Petræa, we
have little difficulty in concluding that the required
species is found in either the *Acacia gummifera*,
or in the *Acacia seyal*, or rather in both. They
both grow abundantly in the valleys of that region
where the Israelites wandered for forty years, and
both supply products which must have rendered
them of much value to the Israelites. The crown,
or rim, of this table was particularly described in
the lectures of the day as being common to it, as
well as the ark of the covenant, and the altar of
incense. It consisted of an ornamented border
of gold, as is seen in the lithograph, which was
set round the table to prevent anything from
falling from it, and so becoming polluted. On
this table were placed the twelve loaves of un-
leavened bread, called the presence bread, because
it was perpetually before the face of Jehovah; a
custom which was imitated amongst the heathen,
who had in their temples a similar table, on which
meat and drink were placed in honour of the
gods, as we find in the familiar instance of Bel
and the Dragon, recorded in the Apocrypha of
our Bibles. The twelve loaves of shewbread in
the tabernacle were baked in moulds by the
priests; and some say they were marked with the
names of the twelve tribes of Israel; but there is

no authority for this conjecture in the sacred writings. They were consecrated with incense, and being placed on vessels of gold, were renewed every sabbath-day. Josephus affirms, that a cup of incense was placed on each stack of bread, as is represented in the figure before us.

The mystical and symbolical meaning of this utensil is thus explained : some understand by it the holy scriptures, and interpret the four rings by which it was carried, when removed from one place to another, the four evangelists, by whom the gospel of Christ is carried, as it were, from nation to nation, till it becomes universal; while others compare the twelve loaves to the twelve months ; and others think the table a symbol of the earth, and the loaves to the fruits thereof. But these interpretations are too fanciful. The table was a symbol of the family of Christ-Jehovah, and the loaves of the true bread of life which that great Being has furnished to his faithful followers. By the incense upon the bread, we are to understand that the preaching of the word ought to be consecrated by prayer and thanksgiving, that we may be divinely incited to the practice of moral and social virtue.

We now come to the consideration of the pot of manna, and the rod of Aaron that budded. It is well known that the manna was given by Jehovah as food for his people in the barren desert, which was called by David [18] " the bread

---

[18] Psalm lxxviii. 9. The Greeks called it *aeromeli*, aerial honey, and the Bedouins use it still for the same purposes as

of angels," as some think, because it was a type of Christ, who was the true bread of life both to angels and to men. The manna was a white, transparent globule, of the size of a coriander seed, and tasted like wafers made with honey, and flavoured with olive oil.[19] A vessel of this pure substance was directed to be laid up before the testimony, as a perpetual memento of the miraculous sustenance of so great a body of people for forty years in a sterile wilderness; and it will be remembered that when they came out of Egypt they numbered three millions of souls. The form of this vessel has been represented like an urn, with a lid or cover; and thus it is depicted on Samaritan medals.

The manna is denominated by St. Paul,[20] "spiritual meat;" whence Christians have considered it as a type of Christ; and for these plain reasons, because, as Jehovah, whom we have already seen identified with the Redeemer of mankind, had compassion on his chosen people when they were famishing in a region where no food was to be had; so the same holy Being had compassion on mankind, when they were in a state of spiritual destitution, and gave his body and blood as a nourishment for their hungry souls.

honey, and regard it as a luxury; but if taken in any large quantity, it is said to prove a mild laxative.

[19] Numb. xxiii. 21. Niebuhr, and Father Pinolo, when describing that of California, which falls, as is supposed, with the dew, says, that without the whiteness of refined sugar, it has all its sweetness.

[20] 1 Cor. x. 3.

In sending forth the manna, Jehovah displayed his tender love towards his people—but much more so when he came in human form to seek and to save those which were lost. He gave them the manna for forty years to teach them obedience under the law—and he has given us his gospel, with a promise of everlasting life to those who should obey its precepts and observe its laws. The coincidences between the manna and Jesus Christ are too numerous to be overlooked, and too important to be despised. He himself drew the first parallel when he said to the Jews—"I am the bread of life. Your fathers did eat manna in the wilderness, and are dead. This is the bread which cometh down from heaven, that a man may eat thereof and not die. I am the living bread which came down from heaven. If any man eat of this bread, he shall live for ever; and the bread that I will give is my flesh, which I will give for the life of the world." [21]

Of the properties and qualities of the manna, the following symbolical coincidences were noticed. The manna was small, but of great virtue; and Christ, though appearing of low degree, possessed unlimited power. The manna was white, the emblem of purity; and Christ was accordingly

[21] John vi. 48—51. On this subject Origen expatiates on the excellency of the Christian Sabbath above that of the Jews, proving that the manna began first to fall upon that day. His words are these:—"If the manna were gathered six days together, as the Scripture saith, and ceased upon the seventh, which is the Sabbath, it evidently began on the first day, which is our Sunday."

pure and spotless. To prepare the manna for use, it had to be beaten and bruised in a mortar —Christ was in like manner beaten and bruised for our iniquities. The manna came from heaven —so did Christ. It was sweet and pleasant to the palate—Christ is sweet and pleasant to the soul. It fell from on high like dew, as Christ imparts his grace and spirit. The manna was supplied till the Israelites entered the promised land; and Christ will supply his church with grace and his Holy Spirit,[22] till the heavenly Canaan shall be opened to all true believers.

The rod of Aaron that budded, and put forth blossoms, and yielded ripe almonds, as a miraculous attestation of his authority, was also ordered to be preserved as a visible testimony of the fact; and the Jews are of opinion that it retained its leaves and fruit to the last, which is indeed extremely probable, else the evidence of the miracle would be defective; and hence it is displayed in a florescent state on our Tracing-board. These two symbols of memorable events in the Jewish history were preserved in the Most Holy Place, *beside* the Ark of the Covenant, and not *in* it, as some have been led to imagine from the words of St. Paul, Heb. ix. 4. They were, however, within the Oracle, and therefore have been characteristically placed, in the drawing before

[22] Referred to in our present Royal Arch Lecture as the *anima mundi*, or the Soul of the world; although I am very much inclined to believe that such an appropriation verges on Materialism, if not Pantheism.

us, beneath the arch where the holy Shekinah is symbolized by the sun, that darts its rays obliquely through the arch, because, according to a Masonic tradition, " the height of the sun at Jerusalem on the ————— was 58°, which formed an angle with the horizon, and caused ————." " Now," says Dr. Kellet,[23] " it is not more odd than true, *quod Sol in nube, Deus in carne;* God in the flesh is like the sunne in a cloud. When Christ was first brought into the temple, the prophetical spirit came upon Simeon; and of extraordinary thanksgiving upon Anna. Was the presence of God in a cloud glorious in the first temple? Much more was the presence of Jehovah in Christ, of Christ in a cloud, superabundantly glorious. A cloud overshadowed them; and a voice out of the cloud said, this is my beloved Son. Againe, was the presence of God *in fulgore,* in brightnesse, such a great priviledge of the first temple? Certainly, the presence of Jehovah in Christ, who was the brightnesse of his glory, and the expresse image of his person, upholding all things by the Word of his power, was much more illustrious and glorious; and the presence of Christ in the bright cloud, when his face did shine as the sun, and his raiment was white as the light, was much more resplendent."

The censer of incense which occupies the upper right-hand corner of the lithograph, surmounted by a rainbow, or halo of light, is a representation

[23] Tricœn. Christi, p. 114.

of the altar of incense, which was made of the
acacia covered with beaten gold. In form it was
a double cube, and had a crown or rim like the
table of shewbread running round its upper
surface. It was of small dimensions, being only
1½ feet square, and three feet high, with elevations
at each corner called horns. The figure in our
drawing represents merely the censer that was
placed upon the altar, in which the incense was
actually burned, in allusion to the words of St.
Paul, Heb. ix. 4; although we have no warrant
in the Jewish writings that such a vessel was
used, for the authority is exclusively Christian.

This altar or censer was placed close to the
veil which separated the holy from the most holy
place, that the incense might penetrate into the
latter; and for this reason, perhaps, it was that
St. Paul attributes it to the innermost room. It
was an emblem or type of Christ, through whom
we offer the incense of our prayers. The acacia
and gold of which the altar was composed, referred
to his human and divine nature; the crown to his
regal dignity; and the horns to his power. As
no incense could be offered but upon this altar,
so no prayers will be accepted but those that are
offered through Christ. The incense was offered
every morning and evening, and our prayers
ought to ascend to the throne of grace at the
same periods. The halo or rainbow which appears
to overshadow the censer, refers to a passage in
the Book of Revelation, which says—"And
another angel came and stood at the altar having

a golden censer; and there was given unto him much incense, that he should offer it with the prayers of all saints upon the golden altar which was before the throne. And *the smoke of the incense* which came with the prayers of the saints *ascended up before God* out of the angel's hand."[24]

I have now redeemed my pledge in the title-page, by conducting the reader quietly, and I trust pleasantly, from the very earliest germ of the Royal Arch, through its different phases and ramifications to its present improved state, as an order well worthy the acceptance of a highly educated generation; including an intelligible account of the intermediate Degrees, as they were practised by the inventors, although now obsolete; and I think I may fairly anticipate the approval of my brethren and companions. Should it however be the decision of the Craft that I have failed, I can only say it must be attributed to misfortune rather than fault; for I have spared no pains to arrive at the true solution of its problematical origin, which has been a desideratum amongst the fraternity for the last half-century at the least. I have not only diligently perused all the scanty evidences which remain in Europe and America, but have deliberately tested their value; and I am not conscious of any error in my conclusions. Hence I can confidently place this work before the Masonic public in the assured

---

[24] Rev. viii. 3, 4.

hope of having rendered an acceptable service to the Craft at large, wheresoever dispersed under the lofty canopy of heaven.

It will not be denied that the seceding brethren, with the assistance of the accomplished Bro., the Chevalier Ramsay, displayed considerable ingenuity in the concoction of their new degrees, which they dignified with the appellation of ANCIENT MASONRY, and succeeded in establishing that doubtful fact, not only amongst the brethren in Scotland and Ireland, but in every other part of the world, as a permanent distinction. Yet it is gratifying to find that amidst all their innovations, they were careful to preserve and retain that sublime reference to JEHOVAH, as T. G. A. O. T. U., which formed a principal element in the Constitutions of Athelstan, was renewed at the revival in 1717, and still animates our improved system of Freemasonry.

I conclude in the words of a well-known invocation. "May the Order, which is founded on the sublime basis of religion and virtue, rise superior to opposition — firm in conscious rectitude, like the bleak mountain which bares its breast with dignified composure to every tempest, and fearlessly presents its bosom to the midnight storm. May it remain a perfect monument of Wisdom, Strength, and Beauty, which ages cannot obliterate nor adversity decay; and may the beauties of Freemasonry be driven by every tempest, and wafted by every breeze, until it shall arrive at the most distant regions of the earth, where civilization is known ; and may the blessing of the Most High be upon all our brethren and companions, and remain with them for evermore. So mote it be."

THE END.

WYMAN AND SONS, PRINTERS, GREAT QUEEN STREET, LONDON.